WALKING IN THE ARDENNES

About the Author

After a short-service commission in the Army, Jeff Williams trained in paediatric medicine and subsequently worked as a consultant paediatrician at a hospital in North Wales for 30 years. During that time he wrote walking and climbing guides for the Stubai, Silvretta and Ötztal Alps. In 2010 *Walking in the Drakensberg* was published by Cicerone.

After retirement Jeff trained as a safari guide in South Africa and currently teaches newly qualified guides the dark art of approaching dangerous animals on foot with clients.

When he is at home in North Wales he lectures on safari guiding and walking in the areas covered by his publications.

Other Cicerone guides by the author
Walking in the Drakensberg

WALKING IN THE ARDENNES

by Jeff Williams

2 POLICE SQUARE, MILNTHORPE, CUMBRIA LA7 7PY
www.cicerone.co.uk

First edition 2014
ISBN: 978 1 85284 686 2

Printed in China on behalf of Latitude Press Ltd
A catalogue record for this book is available from the British Library
Base mapping supplied by Sara Hodges using information © Open Street Map

All photographs are by Maryann Williams except for a few taken by the author
and the following: the Maison du Tourisme in Bouillon kindly provided the
photograph used in 'Early guides to the Ardennes' in the Introduction; I am
grateful to Les Amis de l'Ermite de Resteigne for permission to use the plates in
Walk 28; and the photograph of the chapelle in Walk 32 is copyright Monsieur
O Lefèvre and was provided by the Syndicat d'Initiative at La Roche-en-Ardenne.

Dedication

This book is dedicated to my children Nikki, Christopher, Kate and Jeremy,
of whom I am immensely proud and whose achievements I universally
admire. They and their families have made an old guy's life so much more
complete. They missed out on a dedication in the last book, superseded by the
grandchildren. However, the arrival of a seventh grandchild has complicated
matters so I hope they will forgive me for including George here too.
I love you all very much.

Advice to Readers

While every effort is made by our authors to ensure the accuracy of
guidebooks as they go to print, changes can occur during the lifetime of an
edition. If we know of any, there will be an Updates tab on this book's page
on the Cicerone website (www.cicerone.co.uk), so please check before
planning your trip. We also advise that you check information about such
things as transport, accommodation and shops locally. Even rights of way
can be altered over time. We are always grateful for information about
any discrepancies between a guidebook and the facts on the ground, sent
by email to info@cicerone.co.uk or by post to Cicerone, 2 Police Square,
Milnthorpe LA7 7PY, United Kingdom.

Front cover: Château de Walzin (Walk 25)

CONTENTS

Acknowledgements

The publishing team at Cicerone have, as ever, been very supportive and encouraging, but special mention should go to Clare whose cartographic endeavours, help and advice went far beyond the norm.

I recently had the awkward duty of pointing out a large number of errors in a textbook that had clearly not passed through the hands of an experienced editor. Given that good editing is the saviour of many an author I was very fortunate in having Georgia Laval to edit this manuscript. She picked up not just the inevitable typographical errors but also a number of issues of clarity and poverty of information that may save readers confusion and irritation. Importantly for an author, she also was a model of diplomacy.

The gold award for dedication and steadfastness under occasional sniper fire from the author, in an otherwise extraordinarily busy life, goes together with a large debt of gratitude to my wife Maryann. She took virtually all the photographs, did almost all the walks and subsequently organized the digital images so that we could access them quickly and easily. To that add the most arduous but important task of the lot: reading the script and tactfully pointing out errors of commission or omission and grammatical weaknesses, as well as offering suggestions to improve readability. High five MA.

Rural tranquillity (Walk 3)

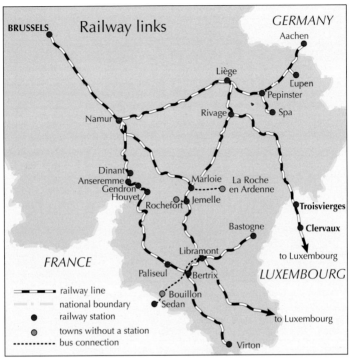

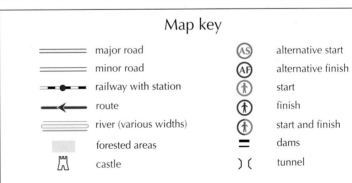

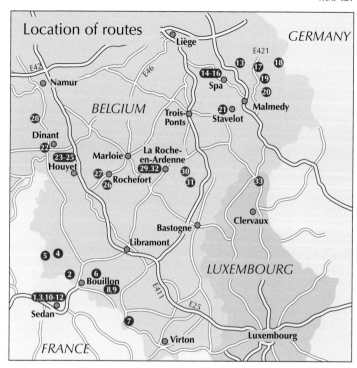

Location of routes

N810 / D977	road numbers (nationale/ départmental)	(M) monument
- - - - - - - -	canoe route	♣ arboretum
- - - - - - - -	track	♦† church/cross
— · — · —	national boundary	* viewpoint
· · · · · · · ·	alternative route	• landmark
	built-up areas	■ dwelling/building
		⊞ cemetery

T	tower
O	dolmen
▨	fenland

Colourful houses along the Ourthe (La Roche-en-Ardenne)

INTRODUCTION

Walking is the perfect way of moving if you want to see into the life of things. It is the one way of freedom. If you go to a place on anything but your own feet you are taken there too fast and miss a thousand delicate joys that were waiting for you by the wayside.

Elizabeth von Arnim (1866–1941)

Consider a region of extensive and beautiful oak and beech forests, of rolling green hills dividing the sometimes steep-sided and deep river valleys, often with castles perched on improbable heights. Add to that a wide choice of activities including vast opportunities for good, straightforward walks, kayaking, biking, horse riding and fishing, all within a four-hour drive of the Channel coast, and you have the Ardennes.

Situated primarily in Belgium and the Grand Duchy of Luxembourg but extending into France, the Ardennes has a great deal to offer the active visitor, especially given its attractive villages (often at the water's edge), good range of accommodation, excellent food and internationally renowned beer.

The military history of the end of World War II in this area – the so-called Battle of the Bulge – is a bonus for many visitors. There are some

A classic leafy walk in the Ardennes (Walk 27)

excellent museums, as well as memorabilia including tanks and artillery pieces popping up all over the place.

GEOGRAPHY

The Ardennes lies within the Belgian region of Wallonia and its constituent provinces of Liège, Namur and Luxembourg. This latter province is easily confused with the country of the same name, so for clarification the **country** will be referred to in this book as the Grand Duchy of Luxembourg (or simply Grand Duchy) – its formal title. Except for two brief incursions, the walks in this guidebook do not include the French département of Ardennes just to the south.

Belgium is one and a half times larger than Wales and about the size of Maryland in the United States. It is very much a country with two principal identities, although it is politically divided into three autonomous regions with four languages. The densely populated northern half of the country is **Flanders**, where the majority of people are Flemish and speak a language very similar to Dutch, albeit in a number of dialects. (Although Flemish is closely related to Dutch it is distinct enough for some Dutch films to have Flemish subtitles – although that may be more political statement than linguistic necessity.) This region is urban Belgium with some beautiful towns but a rather bland landscape, and little in the way of hills.

The southern half of Belgium is **Wallonia** where, in the main, French is spoken. The people refer to themselves as Belgian rather than Walloon. Walloon, a language similar to

Typical Ardennes upland near Trois Points (Walk 21)

French, was the norm until the mid-20th century, but fewer and fewer young people speak it now, preferring French. A survey in 1989 suggested only 17 per cent of people in the region spoke the language well and only 10 per cent used it exclusively. The only other places where it's possible to hear Walloon spoken are around the French town of Givet (close to the Belgian border) and, extraordinarily, in some villages in the US state of Wisconsin.

Belgium's third region is the so-called and very small **Brussels Capital Region**, which is officially bilingual but where French predominates. Finally, there are German-speaking communities in the part of Wallonia known as the Cantons de l'Est – an area ceded to Belgium from Germany by the Treaty of Versailles after World War I, including the towns of Malmedy, Sankt Vith and Eupen. Outside the main cities it is uncommon to find much English spoken, although larger hotels are an exception.

GEOLOGY

Many areas of the Ardennes consist of karst, porous limestone, often tunnelled by streams and dissolved by rain and any acidic components it may contain. This has created large cavern systems that often contain lakes, underground streams and extraordinary formations of stalagmites and stalactites – which have become major tourist attractions throughout the area. Perhaps the most famous is the one at Han-sur-Lesse which, together with its close neighbour the Grotte de Lorette

Stunning stalactite, Grotte de Lorette at Rochefort (Walk 27)

at Rochefort, attracts vast numbers of visitors, particularly at peak holiday times (see Walk 27).

The Hautes Fagnes is an elevated marsh and bog-covered area in the northeast of Belgium. It's beyond the scope of this book to discuss at length the origins of this incredible ecosystem and its almost lunar appearance when seen from the air, but its many circular depressions known as *lithalsas*, originally thought to be the result of human activity over 2000 years ago, are now accepted as a natural phenomenon caused by a geological process about 12,000 years ago at the end of the last glaciation. They are very unusual in Belgium – or anywhere else at this latitude – and are best seen on Malchamps Fagne, south of Spa (see Walk 14).

WORLD WAR II AND THE ARDENNES

All was peaceful; farmers in the fields along the road were ploughing for the winter fallow, and some were taking in the winter harvest, cattle were grazing lazily…

So wrote Robert E Merriam in December 1944, just before the Battle of the Bulge (in *The Battle of the Ardennes*, Souvenir Press, 1958). No account of the Ardennes would be complete without some discussion of the events of December 1944 and January 1945.

German forces attacked through the Ardennes in World War I and again during the 1940 invasion of France. But the wholesale destruction

A Sherman tank outside the military museum in Diekirch (Sentier du Nord, Stage 6)

of villages and towns in parts of the Ardennes belonged almost exclusively to the time of the German offensive of December 1944, and the operation named *Unternehmen Wacht am Rhein* (Operation Guard on the Rhine, suggesting a defensive posture and used to mislead Allied intelligence) – a name that was changed just before the start date of 16 December to *Unternehmen Herbstnebel* (Operation Autumn Mist). To most British and US readers it is known as the Battle of the Bulge.

At that point of the war the Ardennes was considered a backwater by Allied commanders at all levels; a place to rest exhausted US combat units and to provide untried US recruits with a relatively gentle introduction to the Western Front.

After all, Germany was on its last legs, with apparently insufficient troops for further offensive operations; Allied air support was overwhelming and the thickly forested and hilly Ardennes was considered an outrageously unlikely place for an attack. Historically this was poor thinking: in 1914, and again in 1940, the German army had attacked through the 'impenetrable' Ardennes.

The aim of the German counteroffensive was to drive a wedge between the largely British forces to the north and US forces to the south, cross the river Meuse at Huy and Andenne and ultimately capture the pivotal port of Antwerp. This might also have had the effect of encircling and capturing large numbers of Allied troops. However, besides delaying the

RAF war grave and remains of a Lockheed Hudson near Maulusmühle (Sentier du Nord, Stage 2)

inevitable and regaining the initiative for a while, it was totally implausible to expect that the operation would radically change the outcome of the war. In the event, even with temporary local manpower and tank superiority – as well as complete surprise – the attack never achieved its objectives. Partly this was due, in some places, to truly heroic resistance by elements of the US forces, on whom the might of the attack fell, but it was also down to significant resupply problems (notably of fuel for the armour), the Allied air superiority that came with improving weather and the awful condition of the snow-covered tracks and roads for non-tracked vehicles.

By mid-January the German forces were retiring in disarray, almost back to their start points. The Ardennes had been fought over twice in about four weeks and the devastation, as well as loss of life both civilian and military, was considerable. So in most cases the villages and towns you see today are post-war in origin, although in many cases restored in an attractive and faithful manner.

Many places – notably La Roche-en-Ardenne, Bastogne and Diekirch (in Luxembourg) – have well-developed and informative military museums dedicated to the events of the winter campaign of 1944–45, and all over the region there are tanks, smaller museums and other memorabilia to supplement the all-too inevitable and poignant war memorials. La Gleize is a good example with a museum that is very focussed on the events leading up to the pitched battle in and around the village – the furthest penetration of the Kampfgruppe commanded by Lt Col Joachim Peiper, part of the 1st SS Panzer Division.

PLANTS AND WILDLIFE

The Ardennes is rightly famous for its forests. The majority are deciduous, primarily of beech and oak with a sprinkling of birch. Inevitably there are spruce plantations too, although the largest concentration of these is in the Hautes Fagnes area where there are also oak, alder, hazel and large numbers of birch. Those of a botanical persuasion will find the Hautes Fagnes area particularly rewarding with its specialised marsh and bog plants. Plants to look out for are bog asphodel (*Narthecium ossifragum*), moss orchid (*Dactylorhiza maculata*), bogbean (*Menyanthes trifoliata*) and, in particular, round-leaved sundew (*Drosera rotundiflora*) – the tiny carnivorous plant that enhances its diet with captured insects.

Although there are wild boar, red deer, fallow deer and pine marten in the forests of the region they are rarely seen by tourists. Occasional reports of wild lynx have not been substantiated, although it is possible that escapees and released animals exist. Roe deer are more common and red squirrels ubiquitous.

Purple marshlocks (Comarum palustre) with a small pearl-bordered fritillary

Birdlife is splendid. In spring the beech and oak woods are full of birdsong – mostly the same species as seen in the UK, although it is a delight to hear wood warblers singing every 50m. However, there are some 'specials' including grey-headed, black and middle-spotted woodpeckers; Tengmalm's owl and, up on the Hautes Fagnes, giant eagle owl, a few black grouse and nutcrackers.

FOOD AND DRINK

Belgium is generally famous for its food. Unfortunately, technical details of waffles and chocolate and recommendations of eating establishments are beyond the scope of this guide. However, given that Walk 7 includes a visit to a monastery where beer is brewed, a specific note on Trappist beers is warranted.

The Trappist order originated from the Cistercian monastery of La Trappe in Normandy. Although the brewing of beer in monasteries has existed in Europe over many centuries, there are strict criteria governing the use of the label 'Trappist beer'. Indeed it is confined to just eight monasteries in Europe, six of which are in Belgium, two of these (Rochefort and Orval) being in the Ardennes. The two most important criteria for qualification are that the brewing must be undertaken within the walls of the monastery, either by the monks or directly under their supervision, and that the proceeds must be used for the living expenses of the monks, maintenance of the buildings and grounds or given to charity.

A typical example is the Abbaye Notre-Dame de Saint-Rémy 2km north of Rochefort, where only about

Orval Abbey Trappist beer sign with the abbey emblem (Walk 7)

15 monks are in residence. It boasts the longest history of Trappist brewing, dating back to 1595, and the water used in the process is drawn from a well inside the abbey. There are three strengths of beer produced: 7.5 per cent ABV (alcohol by volume), 9.2 per cent ABV and 11.3 per cent ABV, misleadingly labelled '6', '8' and '10' respectively. Considering that over 97 per cent of British 'bitter' beer sold in pubs is less than 4.2per cent ABV it would be wise to remember, when quaffing a couple of bottles of Rochefort 10, that it is likely to be about three times as strong as most people's usual tipple. Be warned!

EARLY GUIDES TO THE ARDENNES

The first English-language guide to the Ardennes was written by Percy Lindley, a prolific author whose books include *Walks in Epping Forest* (1885), *Walks in Holland* (1889) and *The Great Eastern Railway Guide to the Continent* (1902). *Walks in the Ardennes* – subtitled *Cycling, driving, boating, by rail and on foot (with some fishing and shooting notes)* – was published around 1890.

HOW TIMES CHANGE: AN EXCERPT FROM PERCY LINDLEY'S WALKS IN THE ARDENNES

Passport – In Belgium it is quite unnecessary but as some Ardennes tours cross and re-cross the French and German frontiers it may be as well to carry one. A passport is issued on application to the Foreign Office or your banker will save you the trouble.

Time – Antwerp and Brussels time is 18 minutes in advance of English.

Letters – Can be sent from home to care of 'Poste Restante' at any place and should be legibly addressed and the 'Esquire' omitted. Show your visiting card on applying for letters.

Pont de France (Bouillon) with train, date unknown. The tunnel is now a road (Walk 1)

Inevitably, in the last 120 years much has changed in the landscape, as seen particularly in agricultural practices but most notably in the villages. Almost all were at the very least hugely damaged, and in some instances completely destroyed, during the fighting after the German army offensive of December 1944. But such is the rural nature of the Ardennes that I suspect if Percy Lindley had the opportunity of repeating his travels today, he would find much of it is recognisable (although the metalled roads and motorised transport would doubtless surprise and possibly dismay him). There is also a fascinating account of a journey through the Ardennes in 1880 written by Katharine Macquoid (*In the Ardennes*, Chatto & Windus, 1880) but this is not strictly a guidebook. From time to time observations from these earlier books are included in this guide to point up the contrast with the present day.

SCOPE OF THIS GUIDE

This book can only give a flavour of the walking that is available in the Ardennes. Such is the number of possible routes it would be a near-impossible task to cover much more. Each town (and many villages) boasts a tourist office where it is possible to obtain an extensive list of walks suitable for all levels of ability and enthusiasm. For this reason the walks described in this guide are based around five centres in Belgium. In addition there is a long-distance path in the Grand Duchy – the Sentier du Nord – divided into six manageable walks that can all be accessed easily by train.

Horse riding in the forest above Poupehan near the Chaire à Prêcher (Walk 2)

The selection of routes is always difficult and necessarily reflects the preferences of the writer. Wherever possible these are walks with a purpose, but there has also been a determined attempt to limit road-walking to an absolute minimum (although in some instances stretches of tar are unavoidable). There will be many, many walks in other centres, much-loved by others, that are not included here, but tough choices had to be made in order to keep the guide to a manageable size. The fact that over 50 per cent of the walks are in the areas of Bouillon and Spa/Hautes Fagnes reflects the quality of these walking centres.

The challenges of ascent are never too great, given that much of the high ground is between 350m and 500m – although it does rise to over 650m in the Hautes Fagnes.

If, rather than day walks, long-distance footpaths are more your cup of tea, the Ardennes is loaded with them, with a particularly high concentration in the Grand Duchy of Luxembourg. All have the prefix GR (*Sentiers de Grande Randonnées* in French; *Grote Routepaden* in Flemish/Dutch) and most have a Topo-guide that can be purchased in local shops. Special mention should be made of GR14 (Sentier de l'Ardenne), which traverses the area from northeast to southwest, starting in Malmedy and finishing in Sedan in France. It is 221km in length, quite well waymarked and passes through some key 'must-visit' towns in the Ardennes, notably La Roche en Ardenne and Bouillon. Walk 1 and Walk 32 in the book make use of sections of this GR.

GETTING THERE

One of the great attractions of Belgium for British visitors is its proximity to the UK. Almost any of the French or Belgian ports provide good and quite speedy access to the Ardennes, so seeking the sharpest fare in this competitive market is worthwhile. Although at the time of writing there are car ferries from Dover to Dunkirk and Ramsgate to Ostend it is usually quickest to travel via Calais, the crossing time being shorter and services more frequent (with three competing carriers in 2014). Precise directions from the channel ports depend on your destination.

You can fly to Brussels from most major UK airports and then either hire a car or continue by train. Rail connections from London to Brussels are also good and it is possible, though not straightforward, to tailor a walking holiday to an arrival by train with or without local buses. For rail access to the centres featured in this book there are stations at Dinant (for the lower Lesse valley) and Spa in Belgium as well as Clervaux in the Grand Duchy of Luxembourg. La Roche-en-Ardenne can be reached by bus from Marloie on the Brussels to Grand Duchy line. Malmedy (for the Hautes Fagnes) has a bus service via Stavelot from Trois Ponts station on the Liège to Grand Duchy line. Bouillon's nearest railhead is Sedan in France but the bus service between the two only runs twice a day, two days a week. However, there is a fairly good connecting service to the station at Libramont on the main Brussels to Grand Duchy railway. See Appendix B for details of websites offering

Crossing the river using the railway bridge (Walk 25)

information about rail and bus travel in the region.

Rather predictably, most visitors use a car because it allows much better coverage of the area and is more flexible than using what is often poor local transport provision.

WHEN TO VISIT

You can walk in the Ardennes at almost any time of the year, although given that there are a few resorts boasting cross-country skiing – especially in the Hautes Fagnes – winter walking may prove challenging. In July and particularly August the area is extremely busy and early booking for hotels and campsites is highly recommended. For those who can travel outside school holidays, June and September are ideal months for the best chance of decent weather and more peaceful surroundings. By October many hotels, restaurants and activities are closed.

Generally the weather, rainfall and hours of sunshine are very similar to the Lake District region of the UK, although the Hautes Fagnes can have prolonged periods of mist and rain and the winters there are rather colder, with snow sufficient for cross-country skiing.

ACCOMMODATION

There is a wide choice of places to stay, ranging from quite big-ticket hotels to B&Bs and campsites. You have to search a bit more assiduously for rented accommodation (gîtes), but it is available. Trawling the internet is the most successful tactic, but many

B&B in Lellingen (Sentier du Nord, Stage 4)

sites are in French or Dutch and, as with all internet searches, finding the right information can be challenging. All the towns in the Ardennes have tourist offices, variously called 'Office/Bureau du Tourisme', 'Maison du Tourisme' or 'Syndicat d'Initiative'. All of these have websites and are a good alternative to DIY.

When staying in gîtes it is usually necessary to take your own bed linen and towels, and a travel kettle may be useful. See Appendix B for a list of websites that might help in finding accommodation.

MONEY

Belgian currency is the euro. Most gîtes, B&Bs and many small hotels do not accept credit cards, so to avoid the risks of carrying vast amounts of currency an alternative strategy is required. One option is to use a debit or credit card at an ATM, although withdrawal charges can make this expensive. A cheaper way is to organise a debit-type card (usually known as a 'cash passport') that can be pre-loaded with euros at a more advantageous rate than high street banks offer. This can be limited to euros, carries no transaction cost and is used through an ATM in the same way. A number of foreign exchange and travel companies offer this product and the card purchase in the first instance is free. In some places they can also be used as conventional debit cards, again without a transaction charge. The list of websites in Appendix B includes two companies offering cash passports, but it is an ever-increasing market and a general online search will yield plentiful results.

HEALTH AND SAFETY

If you're a European citizen, don't forget your European Health Insurance Card (EHIC). It is necessary to pay a doctor for treatment, but up to 75 per cent of the fee may be reclaimable on return to the UK, provided you have an official receipt (*attestation de soins donnés*). You can seek a consultation with a specialist hospital doctor by appointment without referral from a family doctor, but direct consultation at higher costs may be more difficult in terms of reimbursement. Accident and Emergency departments are run on the same lines as in the UK. Ambulance charges are non-refundable in Belgium but you may be able to claim reimbursement in the UK.

Remember to take your prescription with you if it's possible that you may require a resupply of regular prescribed medication; most pharmacies will accept these but you will have to pay the whole cost, which may be considerable, and seek reimbursement back in the UK.

Citizens from other countries should check they are covered by their medical insurance before travelling.

Ticks are very small, eight-legged arachnids in the same class as spiders and scorpions. They can't fly or jump

Ixodes ricinus, *the most commonly encountered tick*

but they 'quest'. This tactic involves holding the first pair of legs outstretched, ready to cling on to a passing host (maybe a walker). Although responsible for a veritable raft of diseases, in Belgium the risk they pose is the same as in parts of the UK and the most frequently diagnosed transmitted problem is Lyme disease. In order to reduce this risk there are three recommendations: firstly, after walking in wooded areas you should examine all parts of the body (get a close friend to help if you can) to search for ticks. Secondly, take tick tweezers with you (easy to get in the UK and in pharmacies in the Ardennes) and finally, very importantly, if you have unexplained fevers, rashes, joint pains or any other unexplained symptoms in the weeks following an Ardennes walking

holiday, consult your family doctor. The risks are very low – no higher than in the Scottish Highlands, the New Forest or Norfolk, for example – but the potential problem is important and well worth bearing in mind.

Unfortunately it is true that theft from cars (including 'sac-jacking', where a window is smashed and bags stolen from the car when stopped in traffic) and pickpocketing are not unknown in the larger Belgian towns and cities, so the standard precautions are required.

Hunting is a very popular pastime in Belgium. It is highly regulated and tough tests in theory, weapon safety and marksmanship are strictly enforced. The species that can be hunted include deer and wild boar – typically forest animals – so there is a potential for walker-hunter conflict

Hunting hides are common in forests around the region

in terms of safety during the hunting season. In the Ardennes, for most species, the season is from 1 October to the end of December. At these times it is advisable check locally as to which walking areas should be avoided, although there are normally warning signs in place.

WHAT TO TAKE

The same equipment for walking is required in the Ardennes as in the UK and should include a rucksack, waterproof top, appropriate footwear to cope with mud and water, adequate fluids and some food. A map is essential, ideally in a map case or waterproof bag, and a base-plate compass plus a first aid kit and a survival bag (for injuries rather than for an overnight stay) are strongly recommended. The use of a satellite navigation system en route is fun and informative but it is not vital to have such a device.

You won't forget to take your passport, but remember that you must carry it with you at all times as your official ID. When driving you must also always be in possession of a current and valid licence as well as appropriate evidence of insurance.

MAPS

The whole of Belgium is covered by the 1:50,000 Institut Géographique National (IGN) series which are, in principle, the same as the UK Ordnance Survey maps but of nothing

like the same high-quality graphic representation and readability. Notably, footpaths are very difficult to distinguish and follow. The same organisation produces maps at 1:25,000 and 1:20,000 scale, of similar quality.

For basic holiday planning or for multi-day walks these maps are adequate, but for detailed walking routes the best – indeed the only satisfactory – answer is to purchase local maps at local tourist offices or shops. Given the often limited opening hours of the former, this can throw up interesting situations. For example, in 2012 it was possible to purchase a map of the Ourthe Superieure in Nadrin tourist office, open only from 10.00am at the weekend. However, according to a local lady it was worth trying 'chez le pâtissier' (at the baker's) where, sure enough, a copy was produced with a flourish from under the counter. It is usually impossible to source these local maps in the UK prior to departure.

Generally these local maps are at 1:25,000 scale, although there are variations (1:20,000 being quite common). They vary in size and format from place to place. But even these maps are not without problems for walkers: local walking routes are numbered, and in many instances these numbers obliterate the map's detail. Also, these routes are overprinted on existing paths, tracks and roads, and it is often impossible to determine beforehand which surface you will be walking on. Those who abhor surfaced roads may find this particularly trying. It is also worth bearing in mind that some of the maps do not have a legend, and finally it should be remembered that many of the local maps are 15 years or more out of date. However, it needs to be said that the maps of the Grand Duchy at 1:20,000 scale are good.

On the plus side, details of these walking routes, including length, a severity grading and suggested timings, are sometimes included on the reverse of the map.

The maps contained in this guide are derived from open-source materials and adjusted to reflect the author's experience on the ground. They are not designed as a substitute for a decent map or the ability to interpret it; they are adjunctive particularly to give a speedy visual cue to area and terrain. A compass is a useful tool to add to navigational equipment, being particularly helpful to confirm the direction in which a path or track is running when there is some uncertainty about your precise position.

Finally, active forestry management, necessary though it may be, is the bane of guidebook writers and wayfarers alike. Readers should bear in mind that yesterday's walk through a spruce forest rich with the insistent high-pitched song of goldcrests may be tomorrow's amble through open scrubland or new plantation, filled with the scratchy utterances of common whitethroat.

WAYMARKING

The systems used for marking the very laudable number of maintained paths in the Ardennes are bewilderingly variable. The most frequent methods, though there may be many more, are as follows:

- Path numbers printed on a white plastic background and nailed to a tree or any alternative inanimate object
- Path numbers painted in white or black on a tree
- No path number but a symbol such as a red rectangle or green diamond and so on
- Wooden signposts featuring the name of the next feature on the walk

On occasion the sheer volume of numbers and symbols in one site can be overwhelming.

Fortunately, the traditional red and white GR (*Grande Randonnée*) signs are maintained in the Ardennes, although paradoxically GR routes are often omitted from local maps. A

Typical path sign (but shapes and colours vary)

GR signs: (top) turn left; (bottom) 'not this way'

useful and fairly reliable rule is that if there is no GR sign at a junction of paths then one will appear within about 20m. It may be the conventional red/white or the same covered with the 'not this way' cross.

COMMUNICATIONS

There are few public telephones in the Ardennes compared with UK and most of them only take credit cards. Although there is good mobile phone network coverage, 3G is much less widespread. Some hotels provide wi-fi facilities but private accommodation rarely does so. Internet cafés are uncommon and most tourist offices have no such provision. Those who need to keep in touch with the office,

the stockbroker or even the children need to make alternative provision.

The international dialling code for Belgium is 0032.

The telephone number for emergency services is 112.

THE RAVEL NETWORK

In Belgium about 1200km of old railway track and towpath has been upgraded to create a track for non-motorised wayfarers ranging from cyclists (by far the biggest users) to equestrians. This is known as the RAVeL network (*Réseau Autonome de Voies Lentes*). Walkers also use the facility but the flatness of the terrain and the number of bikes discourages large numbers. There are fun features such as tunnels and viaducts, but given the origins of the network, walking routes would be a there-and-back affair, which generally is unattractive. However, there are two routes in this book that incorporate a short section of RAVeL (Walk 8 and Walk 9).

USING THIS GUIDE

The walks are grouped around five centres in Belgium and one in Luxembourg. It is perfectly feasible to do a walk listed under one centre from another area, such are the small distances involved in the Ardennes, although this would inevitably increase motoring costs.

The information box at the beginning of each walk includes details of the length of the outing, an estimate of the basic time it takes, the expected height gain, which map to take and notes on getting to the start, where best to park a car and what facilities to expect en route.

An estimate of the **time** required for a walk is the trickiest aspect of the description. Different people move at different speeds and indeed these speeds will vary from day to day depending on the weight of backpack, weather conditions, time spent studying surroundings or taking photographs, and many other variables. In this book the stated time is simply how long it took the author to walk the route including all stops for writing notes, taking photographs, slaking thirst and for 'comfort breaks'. But it excludes, for example, picnics, sleeping under hedgerows after liquid lunches, prolonged photographic composition experimentation and birdwatching. These timings will be on the fast side for some walkers and a little slow for others. Comparing your own time for one walk, and extrapolating that for the next, may improve predictive accuracy.

The **length** and **ascent** of each walk were measured on a global positioning system (GPS) device and rounded to the nearest half-kilometre. GPS instruments have inevitable inaccuracies but give a much better estimate than measuring on a map.

No system of **grading** is used in this book because the walks are essentially straightforward, differing only in distance and ascent. Where there are special situations, such as a river crossing or ladders, these are clearly described.

Routes are accompanied by clear, contoured colour maps, and the features shown on these maps are highlighted in bold in the route description to help you read the two together. The route summary table in Appendix A will help you choose a route to suit your location, time slot and ambitions.

The first taste of caillebotis, the wooden walkway (Walk 17)

1 BOUILLON AND
THE RIVER SEMOIS

Frahan villag, sitting in a loop of the Semois (Walk 2)

INTRODUCTION

Bouillon, the administrative centre of the commune of the same name, is a truly historic small town (population 2200) with a magnificent castle as its pièce de resistance. Inevitably it is touristy, often packed on holiday weekends and for most of July and August, but nonetheless it preserves an undeniably vibrant and attractive atmosphere. Hidden it certainly is, partly because you can drive past the town on the N89 without even seeing it and partly because outside Belgium, Holland and the neighbouring part of France most other countries know nothing of it or its river – the beautiful and normally placid Semois. This river, whose source is near Arlon on the Grand Duchy border, runs generally west to cross into France near Bohan (see Walk 5), and 10km later flows into the Meuse. Its exaggerated and often symmetrical horseshoe loops take the meaning of meandering to new heights.

The town has all the expected facilities and a useful internet/wi-fi facility, for those in need, at Papeterie des Ardennes on Quai du Rempart, just down from the Pont de France. There is no camping within the town but lots close by.

Local bus services are poor. There is a good, frequent connection with the nearest railway station at Libramont (connections from Brussels and Liège), but the only other helpful route for walkers is the infrequent service to Sedan.

The idea of a single walk to take in all the good views of the town and castle is an attractive one but would be an unhappy compromise, so Walk 10 and Walk 11 visit recommended sites from which Bouillon can be seen at its best.

BOUILLON CASTLE

As the very prominent focus of the town, a visit to the castle is near mandatory. Certainly it dates back to AD988, probably earlier, and in 1096 was sold by its then owner, Godefroid de Bouillon, to finance his leadership of a crusade to Jerusalem. The fortifications were vastly improved by the famous military engineer Vauban in the late 17th century. It's a superb, evocative and informative castle to visit, and great value. You can climb to the highest keep and descend to the lowest dungeon, see the oubliette and walk in seriously dank underground passages as well as through fortifications within the walls. Buy the cheap English-language mini-guidebook that is essential for the DIY tour. The road tunnel under the castle was originally built for the railway described in Walk 1.

WALK 1
Bouillon to Sedan

Start	Pont de France in Bouillon (22km by road northeast of Sedan)
Finish	Sedan railway station
Distance	24km
Ascent	400m
Time	8hrs
Maps	Carte des promenades du Grand Bouillon (1:25,000); French IGN Carte de Randonnée 3009E – Sedan
Refreshments	Restaurants, cafés, bakery and supermarket in Corbion; all facilities in Bouillon
Access	Ideally arrange a lift or position a car at Sedan station. In 2013 the bus service ran only on Wednesday and Saturday, leaving the station at 6.05pm to arrive in Bouillon at 7.00pm. Check at the tourist office for the latest information. You could also consider taking the 8.45am bus from Bouillon and walking the course in reverse. Otherwise an expensive taxi is the only option.

Quite apart from being an interesting and highly enjoyable trek from Bouillon to finish, if you wish, at a fine, classic château fort, this is also an opportunity to have a taste of GR14, the Sentier de l'Ardenne: a long-distance path of 215km linking Malmedy in the northeast of the country to Sedan just over the French border. There are GR signs all the way, although some are elusive.

From the Pont de France in **Bouillon** either go through the road tunnel under the castle or downstream along the Semois, through the Bastion du Dauphin and Bastion de Bretagne and past Pont de Cordemois (this being the longer but more interesting option). Just a short way SW along N810, the Corbion road, is the route down to the river. Follow the easy riverside track, going past Camping Halliru and continuing on a small path at the water's edge for a further 400m to reach a stone bridge over the Ruisseau des Cornais at its confluence with the Semois.

map continues on
page 34

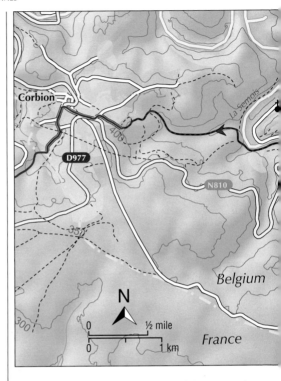

Turn up the valley, keeping right of the stream. The track climbs steadily through deciduous woodland, curving away from and gaining height above the stream to reach a track crossing. Although the GR goes left here it is shorter (although inevitably steeper) to go straight ahead, following the wooden sign to Corbion. Higher up the hill you rejoin the GR before the gradient eases and emerge on a tarred road. Turn left to join the main road and follow it through **Corbion village** to the church at the bottom of the hill (5km).

Opposite the church turn left into the Rue du Chairi and walk along it and its continuation, trending right and downhill to a rough track that, 150m further on, crosses

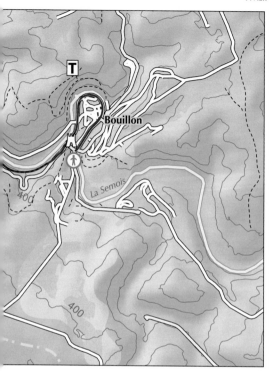

the stream which represents the French frontier. There follows a delightful uphill walk, well signed as a GR, ending in a broad ride with conifers to the left and beech on the right, to join the **N810**.

Turn left and walk along this road for 300m before forking right onto a small forest road that quickly bends right and heads S, surfaced initially but soon easier underfoot. The way ahead seems extraordinarily level; this is because it's the old trackbed of the Bouillon to Sedan railway, featuring occasional cuttings, embankments and gentle gradients compatible with elderly trains *à vapeur* (steam engines).

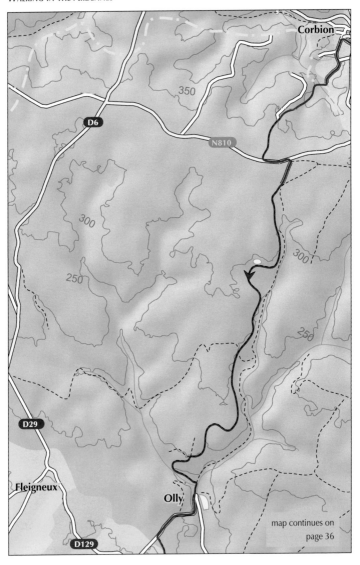

map continues on
page 36

From 1907 a one-metre gauge **local railway** ran from Paliseul, north of Bouillon, through Bouillon to Corbion. In 1910 the connection from Corbion southwards into France was completed, running all the way to Sedan. Essentially the trackbed now lies under the surface of roads and little trace remains, but this walk uses the old and not-so-permanent way for a considerable part of its 21km length. The village of Olly was thus a truly international station, the last stop from Sedan before it crossed over into Belgium to reach Corbion. Passenger traffic ceased in 1935.

Crossing the border

Don't be tempted by lateral paths but march resolutely ahead on this excellent surface, usually with steep ground on the left falling away into the valley of the Givonne. The direction is just W of S almost all the way to the hamlet of Olly, punctuated only by three bends to the W that quickly resume the original heading. On the first of these bends there is a nice pond that is highly suitable for a rest stop.

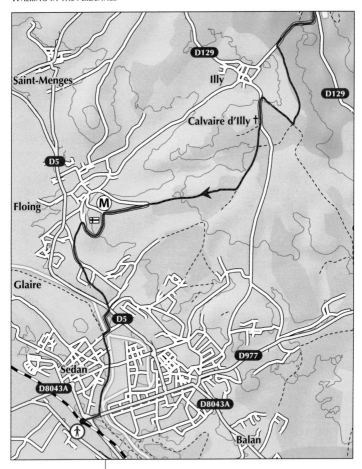

Eventually, just after the third westerly deviation, look out for a sharp left turn that leads quite steeply downhill. A surfaced road announces **Olly**; the old station is still standing but now merely a dilapidated building at the roadside 100m left of the hairpin bend on the D129.

The next leg is testing. Go right and uphill on the **D129** for 850m and then turn left onto a track by some buildings. Follow the track SE, bending SW to a track crossing. Here turn right (unsigned) and soon walk downhill almost to the village of **Illy**. Just before Illy, take a surfaced road left (again unsigned) and go uphill for 350m to a most pleasant picnic area by two crosses, both remembering the Franco-Prussian war of 1870. This is the famous **Calvaire d'Illy**. ▶

Leave the Calvaire on the track between the two roads, going downhill to cross a shallow valley of agricultural land and up the other side to join another track. Turn right and go alongside the wood, under a few trees and up the slope the other side. Take the path that crosses open ground right (W) and then runs down alongside open ground to a fork on a road just after the first house.

The old international station at Olly today

It is much quicker to go straight into Illy on the Olly road and then turn left out of the village to find the Calvaire, but the GR prefers to avoid tarmac.

Beneath the trees of the fork is a German **memorial** honouring the memory of Saxon soldiers of the 94th Infantry Regiment of Weimar, who died hereabouts during and after the battle of 1 September 1870.

Take the left fork and walk down to the splendid and very large memorial dedicated to French African cavalry regiments from 1870 right up to the Algerian troubles of the 1960s. It's a very impressive place. Turn left (S) at the gate to walk just a few metres to the even larger and much more sombre French military cemetery of World War II. Continue downhill, curving round to the NW. ◄ This starts here where, with the Floing church just in sight, it is necessary to spot the tiny path going acutely back left and down between some houses. At the bottom turn left onto a road and after the short hill turn right into Allée de la Hte Gravière. Where this curves right go straight ahead onto an unmade, apparently private, road. It has no GR signs. At the end bend right and go down to a narrow earth path that continues downhill to emerge on a tarred road again by a gate. Follow the road down to where it joins the busy D5 on the edge of **Sedan**.

From here until reaching the banks of the Meuse in Sedan, the navigator has to remain lynx-eyed as the GR markings are infrequent.

To visit the **château fort**, instead of heading directly to the traditional end of the walk at the railway station, turn left onto the D5 and continue straight along Ave General Margueritte to the Place Turenne in the middle of town. The fort is ahead on the left and well signed.

Turn left and cross the D5 at the traffic lights and then turn right into Boulevard Gambetta. This takes a right-angled left turn and leads up to a bridge over the river Meuse (the Pont Neuf). Cross the river and go down steps on the right to reach the riverbank, rather like a tow-path here. Go back under the bridge and walk along the subsidiary canal and under the next bridge to pass two locks. Continue to the third and final bridge and get up to the road on a grassy path. Turning right onto the road reveals Sedan's **railway station** just ahead.

THE BATTLES AT SEDAN

Sedan was the site of one of the most important battles of the Franco-Prussian war of 1870–1871. A large French army, commanded by Marshal MacMahon and accompanied by the Emperor Napoleon III, was attempting to lift the siege of Metz. It was out-manoeuvred by the armies of the Kingdom of Prussia and its allies and cornered at Sedan. The French rear was protected by the fortress of Sedan and an apparently good defensive position set up at the Calvaire d'Illy. However, ultimately the French were surrounded and a rout ensued. After massive casualties Napoleon III called off the counter-attacks and surrendered. He was later exiled in England whilst the German troops besieged, and later took, Paris.

The so-called second battle of Sedan took place between 12 and 15 of May 1940 as part of the German invasion operation 'Fall Gelb' (Plan yellow). The main thrust was to take Sedan, lying as it does on the E bank of the Meuse, to use as a springboard to capture the Meuse bridges. They would use three Panzer Divisions commanded by the highly-thought-of General Heinz Guderian. The French had long believed the Ardennes to be impenetrable to a modern mechanized army and had put few resources into its defence, assuming that an extensive system of concrete bunkers would be sufficient. German troops captured the town itself by nightfall on 12 May without serious opposition. The next phase was to cross the Meuse. Although the preliminary, heavy Luftwaffe bombardment was fairly ineffective in terms of destruction of defensive positions, its effect on the morale of the French troops was considerable and many abandoned their posts. The 1st Panzer Division (1Pz) crossed the river just N of town near Floing on 13 May and made steady progress. The other two divisions met considerable opposition trying to cross the river at Donchery, W of Sedan, and near the village of Wadelincourt. But, thanks to the success of 1 Pz, the bridgehead was established and the breakout to the NW started, the beginning of the end of the 1940 defence of France.

Calvaire d'Illy

WALK 2

Corbion, Crêtes de Frahan, Rochehaut and Corbion

Start/Finish	The church in Corbion, 8km west of Bouillon
Distance	15.5km
Ascent	650m
Time	6–7hrs
Map	Carte des promenades du Grand Bouillon (1:25,000)
Refreshments	Ample opportunity to buy food and drink in Frahan, Rochehaut, Corbion and Poupehan
Access	You can start this sporting challenge in Corbion, Frahan or Rochehaut simply by jumping in at the appropriate point in the text.

This walk combines an interesting mix of woodland walking, ridges, steps, a vertical ladder and, at acceptable water levels, a crossing on foot of the Semois. The section preceding the single ladder encountered en route is signed on the path as 'dangerous and difficult'. After significant rain when the path is muddy it would be very unpleasant and awkward rather than dangerous. Please read the detail in the text. If you don't fancy a ladder then don't do the walk. In its entirety this is a tough but rewarding walk with opportunities for shortening the distance and varying the route.

From the church in Corbion go down the main road, bear right into Croix de Poupehan and after 140m fork left. The route proper starts at the cross a further 120m on, at a three-way split of roads where there are wooden route signs and a barbecue area.

Take the left-hand option, signed for Chaire à Prêcher (The Pulpit) and Frahan. After a short walk past some houses and through an open area the road becomes a track and enters first coniferous and then deciduous woodland. Just at the point where it begins to swing left, walk over to the edge of the escarpment on the right and, a little lower, find the great view down to Poupehan and the river, and seating from which to enjoy it. This is **The Pulpit**.

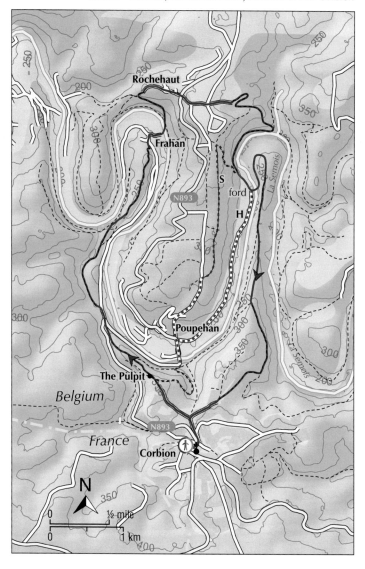

Rochehaut

Frahan

S

ford

H

N893

Poupehan

The Pulpit

Belgium

France

N893

Corbion

N

½ mile

1 km

La Semois

Poupehan from The Pulpit

Do not rejoin the track after this. Instead take a small path that follows the edge downwards NW, winding through the trees and eventually bringing you out on the normal route much lower down. It's just a short distance from there to the crossing of the main road at its sharp bend by the Restaurant Les Croisettes. Go straight over onto a road (signposted Frahan) and after 150m take the track that winds down left into the shallow valley of the tiny Ruisseau du Moulin Joly – the mill referred to being about 1km upstream. Keep the stream on your left and keep right at a junction where the track begins to climb. After 150m there is a fork; although the Crêtes de Frahan is signed uphill and right from here, you should take the left, **downhill**, option. Just before a small bridge and a campsite, look out for the small path (signposted for the GR) that goes up steeply rightwards into woods. This is the first part of the highly enjoyable Crêtes de Frahan traverse. The first landmark is a col on a very narrow isthmus that supports the peninsula at the end of which lies the village of Frahan. Take a moment to look down both sides onto the Semois. You are clearly so high above the river that no oxbow lake could appear here and render Frahan an island community.

Now continue and enjoy the sometimes narrow but never challenging walk, mostly along the crest of the ridge, all the way to Frahan. Its roofs and church spire suddenly appear at your feet as you descend to a particularly good viewpoint. Take note here: you can see the bridge that crosses the river and the track leading up to Rochehaut village, visible disturbingly high up to the north.

As the path reaches **Frahan** turn left to the church. Then keep right down to the end of the road and cross the river on the 1926-built footbridge. There are good picnic sites on both sides of the river here. Turn left following GR signs, climbing all the way to **Rochehaut**. Almost at the top of the hill take the second right at the six-way junction, which takes you up to the main road in 150m. It is just a short uphill walk then to the village centre, but don't miss the view of Frahan, its bridge and its Crêtes, nestling within the loop of the Semois and flanked by high, forested hills.

> **Rochehaut** is a very smart little place that depends largely on tourism, notably trading on its view of a loop in the Semois, for its livelihood. It has cafés, ice cream parlours, restaurants, hotels and home-made food shops as well as three art galleries. It is a good place to stop or start a walk but a bit off the pace for a long stay.

Leave the village by turning right into Rue des Moissons, keeping the church on the left, and at the top of the rise cross the **N893** into the Chemin des Falloises. Keep straight on at the next junction and at the subsequent crossroads where the surface deteriorates. Follow signs for local route 84, go down into the woods, turn right and then fork left. You soon reach a large warning sign for the *Promenade des Échelles* (the ladder walk). 'Difficult and dangerous' are the words used to describe it, and readers of this book must ultimately decide for themselves whether to risk it. The path leads downhill and is decidedly steep in places but never more than

The ladder

awkward (although trickier if muddy). It descends to the river where you turn right. The next section warrants care, the path being steep, narrow and eroded in places, with mild exposure to the river on the left, tree roots to fall over (and hold on to) and short, steep descents where a slip would be easy. Many would agree that the description 'dangerous' is a bit over the top unless you take no care, are physically limited or too young to cope.

. Next you arrive at the ladder. It is more or less vertical and about 6m in height but with comfortably spaced rungs and a guardrail enclosing the top for those descending. It is more a matter of confidence than difficulty and for most people is just a bit of added interest. If in doubt, don't do it and retire with dignity. Note that the new cage at the top makes it impossible to get through with a large rucksack on your back; hauling it is the only remedy.

From the top of the ladder the way is straightforward and the section is completed at a large crag at the top of a steep hill. ▸

This we called the Crag of Confusion as someone has defaced the path signs so as to challenge fellow travellers.

Shortcut via Poupehan (S)

To make the route a bit shorter (by 2km) you can go directly to Poupehan from here by going straight up the hill to the right (W/NW) for a short distance and then taking the first path on the left (path 71). This has the advantage of being wooded and rural almost all the way into the village. Keep more or less S and ignore alternatives that do not bear the legend '71'.

Turn left at the crossing adorned with a modern metal crucifix and emerge in **Poupehan** just 250m above the bridge over the Semois. Continue down the road to the bridge, and from its south side turn left and then continue for 50m before taking the track (60) slanting right up the hillside just before the grotto and shrine. Pass through deciduous woodland for 200m and then take another track that goes up and back left. Continue to gain height until the track levels out and swings right around higher ground. A sharper curve to the right brings you to the incongruously named Pic du Midi (there's no peak and no view to speak of).

Continue upwards for 250m, now on a small path and still in the woodland, to arrive just above the Chaire à Prêcher in a clearing with a path junction. Go uphill along a track (61) that leaves the wooded area, Corbion visible ahead. A crucifix – the Croix de Poupehan – lies at a road/track junction; turn right here. After ignoring a road coming in from the left you quickly arrive at the junction with the main road (N893) in **Corbion**.

Crossing the gué

Expensive electronics such as cameras and mobile phones react badly to immersion in water, so consider footwear rather than a barefoot crossing and some aid to stabilisation such as a staff or walking poles.

From the Crag of Confusion continue the full route by going down very steeply left towards the river on a small, unsigned path and, after 300m, arrive at the **ford** by some holiday homes. The track leads into the river. This is the *Gué de Merleux Han* (the Merleux Han ford). Cross the river here and pick up the path (62) on the other bank.

Using the *gué* (ford) to cross the Semois requires some thought. The river is wide here, often over 30m, though normally in late spring and summer it is acceptably shallow (roughly knee-deep). ◄ If, on arrival at the water's edge, the river is obviously too fast and/or too deep, follow the high water option below. If conditions are marginal, play safe. Otherwise, in good conditions, opt for a preliminary risk assessment that involves nominating or bribing a member of the party to venture carefully into the depths. Safety must always be the watchword. Take no risks and always be prepared to abandon the crossing. Up to knee-depth should be fine in the usual very gentle current, but it's your decision and responsibility. Generally it must be considered a no-no for young children.

High water option (H)
Turn around and head down the track towards Poupehan. It becomes a road and passes many campsites on its journey to the village (2.5km). From there follow the directions in the Shortcut via Poupehan (above) back to Corbion.

On the opposite bank, after 100m take the right fork that leads up into woodland, gradually curving round to head S. **Note The contours on the route map are unreliable here**. You pass the alleged viewpoint 'Rocher des Eperviers' above you on the left but it isn't worth the scramble. The track arrives at a clearing, presenting three route choices; again the map is misleading, but you should take the central track for just 200m to where a small path goes up left. Follow this (currently numbered 62 and 34) as it undulates along or just right of the crest of the narrow ridge.

As you leave the obvious ridge there is another three-way junction; use the left-hand track (routes 34/63/68) that takes the E side of the ridge and, after ignoring a vague track crossing, keep right when another obvious track joins from below left. This leads to a T-junction where, a few metres down to the left, the famous Gros Hêtre (the big beech) still just about stands in its dotage. Keep right at this junction and follow the track all the way up to the cross at **Corbion** where the adventure started.

WALK 3
Bouillon to Poupehan and back

Start	Pont de Cordemois, Bouillon
Alternative Start	Poupehan (if not kayaking)
Finish	Bouillon
Distance	15km kayaking; 7.5km walking
Ascent	170m
Time	3hrs kayaking; 3hrs walking
Map	Carte des promenades du Grand Bouillon (1:25,000)
Refreshments	Restaurants, cafés and shops in Poupehan and Bouillon
Access	An alternative in unsuitable river conditions (or kayak aversion) is to travel to Poupehan by taxi or to get a lift. The bus service is unhelpful. Check with the Bureau du Tourisme beforehand for other suggestions or improvements to public transport. It is possible that the kayak hire company would take a passenger in the coach used to go to Poupehan to return paddlers to the start.
Kayak hire	Semois Kayaks (www.semois-kayaks.be) go downstream. Advance booking is recommended at busy times or out of season (see Appendix B); return transport is provided from Poupehan and they will take a rucksack or a bag for the return trip. No prior kayaking experience is required and safety considerations (swimming ability, wearing a life-jacket etc) are personal decisions. In 2013 the cost was €18 per person.

This adventure involves sequential use of kayak and foot – the best possible ways to experience the river and countryside.

The watery segment starts from the Pont de Cordemois in Bouillon, where can pick up your kayak and leaving your walking gear for the journey back with the hire company. Depending on your fitness, experience and dedication it may take up to 3hrs by kayak to reach Poupehan from Bouillon.

On arrival and after taking refreshment in **Poupehan**, make for the south side of the bridge over the Semois

Kayaks on the Semois

to begin the walk back. Turn left and continue for 50m before taking the track (60) slanting right up the hillside just before the grotto and shrine. Pass through deciduous woodland for 200m and then take another track that goes up and back left. Continue to gain height until the track levels out and swings right around higher ground. A sharper curve to the right brings you to the curiously named Pic du Midi (curious because it is not a peak and the view is unremarkable). Even the attendant bench looks old and tired of its job.

Continue upwards for 250m, now on a small path and still in the woodland, to arrive just above the Chaire à Prêcher (The Pulpit) in a clearing with a path junction. A very small diversion downhill to the edge of the escarpment takes you to the Chaire with its genuinely worthwhile view back down to the village and river.

Go back the few metres to the junction and go uphill along a track (61) that leaves the wooded area, Corbion visible ahead. A crucifix – the Croix de Poupehan – lies at a road/track junction; turn right here. After ignoring a road coming in from the left you quickly arrive at the junction with the main road (N893) in **Corbion**. On the left

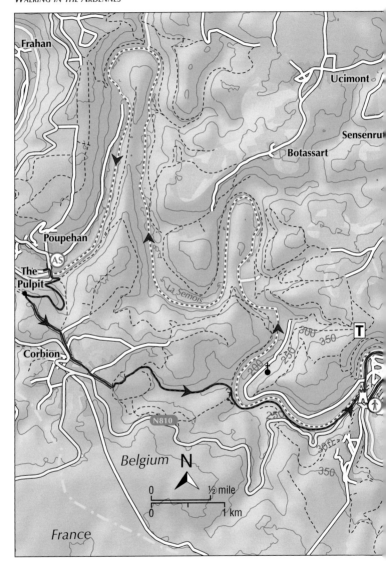

is a narrow road, locally called Ruelle Lolette, which leads up to a public footpath, goes behind the lovely garden of the Hotel des Ardennes and reaches a crossroads. Go straight across and down a track into woodland to a fork. Here the GR signs lead right but it's better to keep left and descend, moderately steeply, to a track crossing at the top of a wide re-entrant and rejoin the GR there. Take the track ahead, which heads off SE on the left side of what becomes a narrow valley and then runs down the left bank of the Ruisseau des Cornais, to arrive at the confluence of that small stream with the **Semois**.

Variant to the top of the Rocher du Pendu
Cross the bridge and turn up rightwards, following a marked path (38) that climbs the 60m to the top of the Rocher du Pendu by well-graded zig-zags. The view downstream over meadows is pleasant, although the Abbaye Notre Dame de Clairefontaine is concealed from sight and upstream lies a large and busy campsite. So as a viewpoint it is disappointing, and apart from the extra height gain there is a 500m-distance penalty for satisfying curiosity.

The direct way back to Bouillon follows the river all the way. Turn upstream, going over the concrete bridge, and follow the riverside path to the entrance to a large campsite. Walk along the riverbank on a good path. On the way there is a shrine to Notre Dame de Lourdes, after which the track is cobbled, allowing worshippers of yesteryear to visit the shrine by carriage. This track is known as the Sentier Ladmirant after a gentleman of the same name.

The track reaches the N810 just 200m before the road tunnel under the castle. Make your way back into **Bouillon** on the riverside or through the tunnel.

WALK 4

Vresse and Membre

Start/Finish	Vresse-sur-Semois
Distance	14.5km
Ascent	400m
Time	5hrs
Map	Vresse-sur-Semois, carte des promenades (1:25,000)
Refreshments	Shops and eateries in Vresse and Membre
Access	Vresse is 21km west of Bouillon by road

The role of the French Resistance in WWII has been extensively publicised. Much less is known of the Belgian resistance movement that, in the Ardennes, was composed largely of local *chasseurs* (hunters) who brought their own persuasively effective skills to guerrilla warfare. This walk visits two relevant sites, including a preserved maquis camp, and later crosses the Pont de Claies – a woven bridge over the Semois.

> *At Membre, a few miles below Alle on the opposite bank, the Semois is especially lovely, and thence to Bohan, where hills, with dark gorges between them, green valleys, and the silver Semois taking its winding way through all, make constant and varied beauty.*
> Katharine Macquoid, *In the Ardennes* (1880)

Vresse-sur-Semois is a pleasant, smart, one-street village with ample parking out of season and an excellent Maison de Tourisme, but, as do all villages around here, it gets very busy in season. Camping opportunities abound and there is accommodation and many restaurants.

From the SW end of the village walk W along the N914 for 100m and then turn right into the Rue de la Chapelle, forking right again at the chapel. The surfaced lane soon peters out into a stony track and, after one hairpin bend, steadies down onto a northerly heading

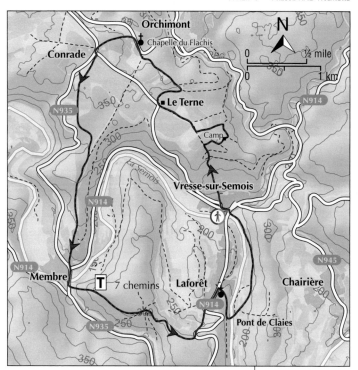

steeply up through woodland. Ignore other options and keep N until the gradient eases at a track junction by the corner of a field. Turn right and walk about 250m over a slight rise and down to a sign. Turn left and go quite steeply down for about 150m to the old Maquis **camp** in a glade at the foot of a small rocky outcrop. The site is very atmospheric.

This is the camp of **Blaireaux**, renovated to its 1944 condition. It was one of over 20 such camps in the Basse-Semois and was never discovered by the German occupying forces, notwithstanding the presence of a Panzergrenadier detachment that

The Maquis camp 'Blaireaux' was garrisoned in Vresse and Membre for a time. It has sleeping accommodation, a kitchen, a dining room and even a small chapel, all widely dispersed among the trees. There was also a very discreet telephone connection to a house in Vresse in order to provide an early warning of troop movements.

Leave the camp E, going down to a track junction where there is a signpost for the camp (as most visitors arrive from a nearby road). Turn left (N) and after another left fork go up to a T-junction. Turning right here leads to a surfaced lane in open countryside and down to **Le Terne** farm. Take the track on the right immediately after passing the farm and follow this to the corner of a wood. Here turn left and go down a pleasant and grassy lane with a nice view northeast across a deep valley to the village of **Orchimont**. The key landmark is a complex junction of tracks and a road; keep straight ahead and join the road that is heading NW. Just 300m up the gentle hill lies the **Chapelle du Flachis**.

CHAPELLE DU FLACHIS

Jean Daelemans was a vigorous proponent of resistance against the German occupying forces while studying at university in Louvain (Leuven) and he joined Group D of the Ardennes maquis on the day after his wedding. His wife joined him on 2 September 1944 at Camp Blaireaux. On that day he and others attacked two German vehicles; one was destroyed but the other escaped to raise the alarm at Vresse. The response was swift and violent. A German force burnt the four farms of the hamlet of Conrade and a fierce firefight lasting five hours took place in the area around the crossroads and just south of it. Here Daelemans and one other, Paul Bollingh, were killed.

His widow later arranged for the building of the chapel close to the spot where he died. The door is usually open, but, as the caretaker advised, 'it may need a shoulder m'sieu'. It has a simple table and benches, beautiful stained glass windows and a commemorative plaque for those maquisards of Group D who lost their lives. This is a most worthwhile visit and very moving.

Turn left 150m higher up the road onto a track running through coniferous woodland, and follow this alongside some farm buildings to emerge on the N935 in the tiny hamlet of **Conrade** (the site of the German reprisal detailed above). Turn left and walk a short distance down to a junction where you turn left again, but only for a few metres. Take the track that goes to the right alongside open land and then leads into forest again. Take the left fork at the next junction and go down to a stream in a shallow re-entrant, rising up gradually on the other side. From there it's simply a question of descending to join GR126 on the remains of a Roman road that ran from Cologne to Reims.

Just before reaching the main road at **Membre**, slip down left past the church to arrive in the main street. The bridge over the Semois is ahead; the riverbank on the right is not only easy to access down some steps but also has several refreshment options, from drinks to ice cream, chips to a full lunch. The benches by the river add to its attraction as a rest stop.

To continue the journey, return to the bridge and cross the river. Ignore the road on the left but immediately after the house turn left up into the woods. It's a steep haul up to a **viewing tower** at Roche à Saloru (325m). Leaving there, take the right fork and walk down to a place called **Les 7 Chemins**, where there really is

Pont de Claies

a seven-path junction. Keep straight ahead with steep ground down to the left and soon join the road. Descend around the corner and cut left down a track, passing the hotel La Sapinière, and down into the square of the village of **Laforêt**. Take the road to the right of the church and pass the old communal bathhouse – sadly now in very poor condition – to follow the road's right-hand curve onto a track that leads down to the river. Here is the **Pont de Claies**.

> The word '**claies**' (woven) is the giveaway. This is a style of bridge that is woven and replaced each year in June, having been dismantled in the previous September. Here it is made from hornbeam, the tresses being fixed onto wooden pylons sited in the riverbed. There is no handrail and it's unsuitable for younger children to go it alone – indeed adults need to tread carefully for the enjoyable 30-metre crossing.

Cross the bridge and turn left onto the path leading downstream along the bank back to **Vresse**. The final highlight of this great walk is to cross the lovely, though tiny, Pont Saint Lambert (1774), which takes you across the Petit Fays stream and back into the village.

WALK 5

Bohan and the French frontier

Start/Finish	Bohan village
Distance	12km
Ascent	370m
Time	4hrs
Map	Vresse-sur-Semois, carte des promenades (1:25,000)
Refreshments	Restaurants and shops in Bohan
Access	Bohan is 7km by road west of Vresse and 28km from Bouillon

Bohan is another extremely attractive Semois village, good enough to visit and sit by the river even if you don't want to walk. The walk described here takes in a stretch of the French frontier that in previous times was a notorious haunt of smugglers, and finishes with a splendid view of Bohan from a tower.

In Bohan's main street there is a post with a colour-coded key for each walk; remember the red rectangle for it will be your companion for several kilometres (together with GR signs) as far as the first contact with the French border. Go SW down this street to its end and turn left into Rue du Herdier. Surprisingly, the signage takes you almost into the front doors of a row of cottages and flirts with entering their garage before slipping almost imperceptibly into the forest on a tiny path.

The gradient here is alpine and the 130m up to a large cross (with a view and a welcome bench) is a demanding start. But the Ardennes can never keep this up and the path then stays at exactly the same height for over 3km to the place known as 'Bois Jean'. En route keep right at Roche La Dame and, much later, ignore the old buildings down on the right.

At Bois Jean turn right (NW) and go down steeply to where the path runs along a balcony above the Semois. On the other side of the river lies French soil. A hairpin bend leads the path down to the valley floor at a ford across the Ruisseau du Bois Jean. This was the site of

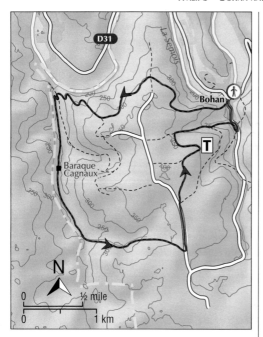

Baraque Gérard, of which no trace remains. Across the
ford lies France and the continuation of the GR.

> Essentially a **baraque** is a very crude dwelling,
> although they were enhanced somewhat over time.
> Baraques were sited near to the Franco-Belgian
> frontier and were the haunts of smugglers, some of
> whom gained national recognition by their exploits
> in spiriting tobacco and coffee across the border.
>   The only surviving baraque on this walk is
> Baraque Cagneaux. In 1855 a Mme Cagnaux-
> Lamotte lived here; the building in its original form
> – and at that time in open ground – survived until
> 1924 when it burned down. There was some res-
> toration in 1980 but even by 1987 photographs
> reveal that vegetation had taken over.

Baraque Cagneaux as it looks today

Now head S on the path that sticks strictly to the valley floor for almost 2km, keeping left of the stream that represents the French border (except for one wet excursion over and back). Occasionally the terrain is reminiscent of border crossing films where the daring smuggler zig-zags desperately across open ground to avoid the fusillade from the French *douaniers* (customs officers), whose dogs are straining at the leash. At other times it's just a tangle of bushes and trees along the water's edge. About 1km from the site of Baraque Gérard are the remains of **Baraque Cagnaux** – broken, derelict and almost hidden in the vegetation that surrounds and grows inside it.

After the 2km along the valley the path rises slightly up to the site of Baraque Léger and then trundles down again. However, this is the moment for a change of direction: the original valley continues S but the path heads E and up a smaller valley on its right side. Initially the going is easy, rising gently through cleared forestry, but all too soon there is a belt of secondary growth – mostly young silver birch just above head-height – that is very

thick (such that at times a machete might be handy). The path is easy to follow but narrow and, after rain, wet and muddy, so it is a considerable relief when mature woodland takes over and brings a better track with it. The gradient gradually eases and a narrow, tarred road in an area called Ansessa makes a welcome appearance. It has been roughly a 170m climb from the frontier.

Turn left onto the road and walk for 700m to a path junction. A track leads NNE, later turning more NE to arrive at what's marked on the map as a viewpoint. In fact it's a tall viewing platform or **tower** (*belvédère*) that is well worth climbing. Afterwards the path leads W before turning into a small re-entrant with a track on the right. Ignore this and walk for a further 200m to join an obviously better-used track running down from the W. Continue downhill on this, passing behind a house to emerge at a bridge over the Ruisseau de Bohan. Follow the road downhill back to **Bohan**.

Bohan from the cross

WALK 6
Dohan and the Semois

Start/Finish	Semois bridge in Dohan, just below the river (parking adjacent)
Distance	16.5km
Ascent	300m
Time	4hr30min
Map	Carte des promenades du Grand Bouillon (1:25,000)
Refreshments	No facilities
Access	Dohan is about 10km east of Bouillon by road

This is a straightforward woodland walk starting and finishing in the small village of Dohan on the bank of the Semois. In May and early June it's alive with birdsong; in autumn the beech and oak trees provide a veritable riot of colour.

From the bridge over the Semois in Dohan, go SE up the N865 in the direction of Herbeumont for about 180m then turn left onto local path 19 (red triangle), signposted 'Promenade de la Dampirée'. This section undulates along and above the river and touches the road just once at a lay-by. There are a couple of benches at viewpoints along the way, including at the Roche de la Dampirée and at a fine position just after the very steep zig-zags that take you up towards the road for the second time.

On reaching the **N865** again do not follow the path 19 signs but cross straight over and take the leftmost of the three paths there. This runs straight, roughly SE, and after about 700m arrives at a crossroads where you turn right, rejoining path 19. This 'shortcut' avoids a stretch of road-walking.

From here the forestry track is fairly level and winds around the hillside through beech, oak, some birch and conifers to emerge on a tarred road at a place known as 'Monument Dubois'. The small stone **memorial** commemorates one Alexandre Dubois, Director-General of Eaux et Forets (although it omits the dates of his reign).

Turn right and go down the tarred road for 150m to the sign for Bois Brulé (the burnt wood). Here fork left onto the forestry track and follow this for about 2km before turning back acutely right (NE) onto a more pleasantly surfaced track. After another 2.5km take the left fork. ▸

After 900m keep left at the next fork and a few metres further on turn sharp left and steeply downhill to reach a lower track. Go straight across this and slightly upwards to a knoll **viewpoint** (Rocher des Clappes).

The right fork leads quickly to the road that connects Monument Dubois to Dohan which, if taken in its entirety, is useful as a shortcut, saving 3km should you so desire.

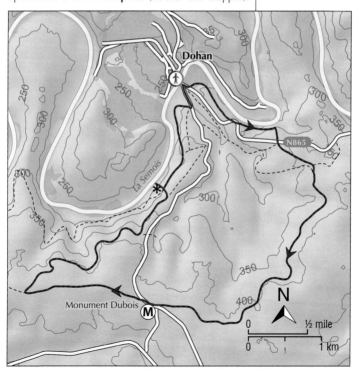

Riverside forest

There is a bench here and, while the outlook is pleasant rather than stunning, it's a nice place for a break before the final push. Go back to the lower track, turn left and after about 250m you rejoin the original path. Of course, if you're 'viewpointed out', omitting this saves a bit of distance and ascent.

This walk has an excellent finish. After a sharp right-hand bend in the track turn left at a sign 'Pte de vue Rocher Lecomte'. The lovely path gives a good view of Dohan at a rocky promontory and then continues down-hill in the same line through the woods to a track by some cottages. Turn right and quickly reach the road; follow this left for just a few metres to complete the circuit at the Semois bridge in **Dohan**.

WALK 7
L'Abbaye Notre-Dame d'Orval

Start/Finish	Close to the Orval abbey entrance
Distance	7km
Ascent	100m
Time	2hrs
Map	French IGN Carte de Randonnée 3110E – Montmédy
Refreshments	Limited facilities in Villers-devant-Orval; beer and cheese available to buy at the abbey
Access	From Bouillon take the N83 east to Florenville and then the N88 southeast to Orval. It is well signposted and there is ample parking.

A visit to a ruined abbey; a tasting of Trappist beer and cheese produced within the holy walls; and a short leg-stretch into nearby France to see both the scene of a war atrocity and an historic café make for a nice, short and possibly calorie-rich rather than calorie-burning day.

The walk from the abbey to Margny is short on spectacular views but longer on history. Start just before the entrance to the abbey on an unsigned track at the corner of woodland. Go gently uphill and over the crest take the small path that curves back leftwards down to the road. This short section is simply to avoid trudging back to the crossroads on the road.

Now follow the **N88** (signposted Virton) along the wall of the lake and continue for about 600m, being careful to look out for traffic on this sometimes busy road. Take a wide track leaving the road right at 90°. This uses what was formerly the dam wall of the Neufmoulin pond, the exit stream of which runs under you and which also represents the Belgian border. So march uphill through a tunnel of trees, possibly whistling the *Marseillaise*, into the French département of Ardennes. You emerge in open ground at a track junction by a picnic table. Go right and shortly afterwards follow this track as it curves

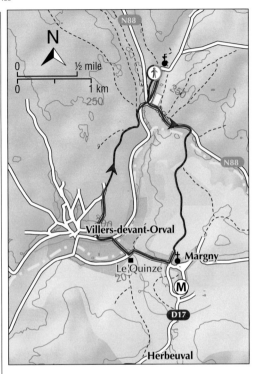

This is agricultural land and in spring and summer skylarks hover and sing overhead.

left towards the village of Margny directly ahead. ◄ You arrive in **Margny** along the appropriately named Chemin d'Orval. The onward route leads down the road right-wards from here.

Make a short diversion into **Margny**. This village of 160 inhabitants would be rather ordinary but for two features: the first, up past the church and to the northeast, is an impressive fortified castle-like house dating from the 17th century. But it's the second that stirs the emotions. On 25 August 1914, following the shooting of a German officer by French soldiers, the entire adult population of the

The martyrs' memorial in Margny

village whose ages ranged from 14 to 73 years were locked up in the church and then shot. A memorial at the end of the short road south of the church commemorates the event, all the more emotive as it was a case of mistaken identity. It was the wrong village – the officer having been killed in the nearby village of Breux.

The surfaced road leads down to cross La Suquette stream. On the left just after the bridge is **Le Quinze** – a French café sitting almost on the frontier, which had its heyday in the 1960s when large numbers of Belgians

Le Quinze café

walked across the border on Sundays to partake of alcoholic beverages forbidden to them in their own country 50m away. Sadly it is now closed.

Turn right and re-cross La Suquette, passing a large house on the left that was built in 1873 and formerly known as 'Le Casino' (meeting place). After a few metres you are treading the border between France and Belgium and only properly pass into Belgium again after crossing the Marche stream with its old mill. This was where the French, in turn, crossed into Belgium to buy coffee, tobacco and other goods that were significantly cheaper there. The creation of the EEC has firmly put paid to such fascinating customs.

Turn left after the bridge into the main street of **Villers-devant-Orval** and then right after the nursing home named after Saint-Jean-Baptiste. Continuing along the main road would take you to the heart of the pleasant village and to the highly recommended hotel built on the site of a castle destroyed by bombing in 1940. Instead, go up the hill to a road junction and 50m beyond that take a track on the right at a crucifix. After the farm buildings this path becomes pleasantly grassy. Follow it, taking the right option whenever it is offered, down to the Villers–Orval road, joined close to the crossroads to complete the circle of the walk. All that remains is 500m back to the **abbey** car park.

ORVAL ABBEY

Founded in 1070, Orval became Cistercian in 1132. Just as it finished a complete rebuild in 1793 it was looted and largely destroyed by anti-religious French revolutionary troops. The ruins of these original buildings were abandoned and eventually, in 1926, the building of the present abbey was commenced. The ruins are well worth a visit, very well organised but audio is only available in French or Dutch. However, the descriptive boards are also in English. You learn not only about the history of the monastery but also of the art of brewing and cheese-making. Indeed, Orval is probably best known for its production of Trappist beer and local cheese, which are both sold in the abbey shop and in a café just up the road.

When the abbey was founded the monks chose the site of a well-reported miracle. The widowed Countess Matilda of Tuscany, who was visiting the area, dropped her wedding ring – which had been given by her deceased husband Godfrey the Hunchback – into a stream. Appalled by the loss, she hastened to a nearby oratory and offered prayers to the Virgin Mary. When she returned to the stream a trout emerged from the water, the ring held in its mouth to return to her. Understandably the Countess was both delighted and amazed and declared that henceforth the valley would be called *Aurea Vallis* (the golden vale). The trout and the golden ring now form the emblem of Orval.

WALK 8
Herbeumont: Viaduct and château

Start/Finish	Herbeumont Château car park
Distance	9km
Ascent	175m
Time	3hrs
Map	Herbeumont, St Medard, Straimont (1:25,000) or Chiny, Florenville, Herbeumont (1:25,000)
Refreshments	Shops and eateries in Herbeumont
Access	Herbeumont is about 27km by road east of Bouillon. From the centre of the village go southwest along Rue des Ponts, then half-left over the old railway bridge into Rue du Château from where the château is signed and where there is a car park.

The delightful village of Herbeumont sits above the Semois and boasts a network of walking trails plus a very fine 13th-century castle which, although like most of its contemporaries is ruined, has been sufficiently well preserved to make for a pleasing visit.

The first of the two walks described from the village (Walk 8) is an abbreviated version of the second (Walk 9) with an added section to create a round trip that is particularly recommended. All the sights of the area south of Herbeumont are here in a vast area of beech and oak forest, honeycombed with paths, on a plateau above the river.

From the château car park, walk back to cross the railway bridge and turn right into Ave des Combattants to go down the hill into the old station and goods yard area, now a caravan and motorhome park. Continue along the trackbed of the **old railway**, crossing the road on a bridge with ornate iron railings, and then onto the viaduct.

The 150m-long **viaduct** spans the Semois that flows peacefully some 38m below. It is available to walkers and cyclists, and although the wire cage is unsightly and slightly spoils the atmosphere, health and safety reasons presumably mandated its construction, especially as there is no parapet.

Herbeumont viaduct, now a walking and cycling route

On the S bank of the river walk along the old embankment for 250m, again crossing the road, then go right onto a surfaced forestry lane at the point where it runs close to the old line. Go uphill for a further 250m to encounter three options: on the left is the continuation of the road, and the right-hand option sees the tarred surface changing to a stony track. Take the middle way – a pleasant path, soon with high earth banks and becoming fairly steep. Keep left at the junction with a wider track, still rising but at a much easier gradient. At a crossroads in a large clearing turn right and continue on this for a little over 800m. Then look out for the turning on the right, unsigned but an obvious path. If the track bends sharply left then you have gone too far and

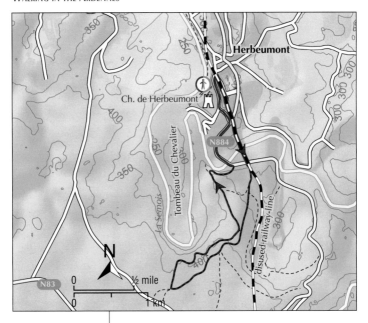

will eventually hit a public road, an obvious catching feature.

The new path, heading roughly N, is part of a GR, although at this point it is badly signed. After roughly 250m the path veers right and there is a deep valley emerging on the left. After another 250m it rises to an excellent viewpoint, well equipped with a seat, a shelter and even a waste bin. A large loop in the Semois lies before you, enclosing the so-called **Tombeau du Chevalier** (the knight's tomb, requiring quite a leap of imagination to visualize it) with the Herbeumont fortress on the hill beyond, just to the left of the village.

Leave to the E, following GR signs (which you will now follow all the way to the main road), and descend to cross a re-entrant before climbing up to the next viewpoint (adorned with just a seat). After 200m is a fork; go left and continue gently downhill as far as a T-junction

with another seat. Again turn left, still losing height, to yet another T-junction, yet another seat, and yet another left turn. Suddenly, 200m lower down, the trees open up and there's a super view of the village, château, river and viaduct, although potential photographic splendour is little enhanced by the caravan site on the river bank. Just below this viewpoint is another shelter for those caught in inclement weather. After ignoring a left fork the GR suddenly dives down sharply to the right and becomes very narrow, with the ground falling steeply away down to the river.

It emerges on the **N884** close to the bridge over the Semois. Cross the river and walk uphill as far as the old railway bridge. Here turn left and walk to a junction, then turn right. Continue uphill past the Chapelle St Roch and quickly arrive at the château **car park**.

Tombeau du Chevalier and Herbeumont castle from the viewpoint

73

WALK 9

Herbeumont: Mortehan, viaduct and the château

Start/Finish	Herbeumont Château car park
Distance	19km
Ascent	380m
Time	6–7hrs
Map	Herbeumont, St Medard & Straimont (1:25,000)
Refreshments	Shops and eateries in Herbeumont
Access	Herbeumont is about 27km by road east of Bouillon. From the centre of the village go southwest along Rue des Ponts, then half-left over the old railway bridge into Rue du Château from where the château is signed and where there is a car park.

This, the second route based on the lovely village of Herbeumont, is quite long and much of it is on GR15 (Ardenne-Eifel). It is only slightly marred by a 3km stretch of road-walking halfway round, although this is a forest lane with virtually no traffic. The start is particularly attractive but you can save more than 1km by using village roads to take you onto the country lane by the railway bridge.

Leave the top of the château car park by the seats and follow a path that takes you downhill through woodland to emerge on a road. Immediately turn back right and continue downhill to arrive at the riverside. It's a lovely, flat walk from here that ends at the official bathing area for the village, which is even equipped with a ramp to avoid having to dive in from the bank. Go up the concrete steps to the road above. Avoid the grassy ride starting opposite; instead walk a few metres right to the next ride. After a lot of rain parts of this can resemble a particularly challenging section of a bog snorkelling course, but persistence wins the day and after 300m it reaches the **N884**, north of the village at the point where it goes under the **old railway**. Go under the bridge and turn left into a country lane.

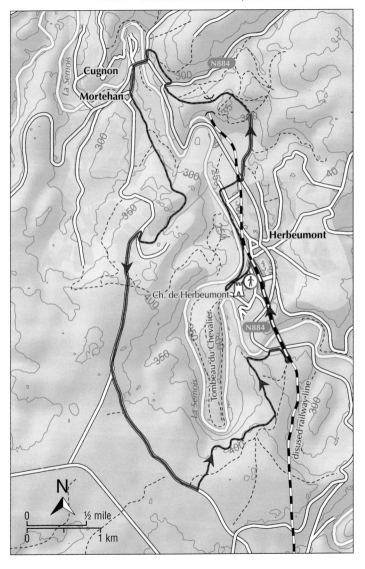

Cugnon

Mortehan

N884

La Semois

300

300

300

350

292

Herbeumont

400

Ch. de Herbeumont

Tombeau du Chevalier

350

N884

400

300

La Semois

disused railway line

N

0   ½ mile
0   1 km

*Fly-fishing on the
Semois*

The lane is very quiet and, after curving left (N), rises steeply. Beyond the last house the road is unsurfaced and leads up to a track junction, the site of a shrine (Chapelle Ste Barbe). Subsequently it turns W (and past what used to be a viewpoint, presumably when the trees were lower – do not follow the red diamond signs off the track) before descending the spur to emerge at the junction of N865 and N884.

Turn right onto the main road and walk E for 100m to find what was probably the old carriage road, going up left and across the hillside to join a small road just north of the Semois road bridge. Pick up the signs of the GR, leading left, to cross the bridge towards the unimpressive village of **Mortehan**. Once across the bridge, turn left up a lane and keep left through the houses to pick up a track. After 400m the track jinks left to cross a tiny stream; just a few paces further take the very steep earth path on the right that goes up a spur. This trends left of the higher ground, although it continues on the same heading, and reaches a gate in a deer fence. After crossing the head of a re-entrant it's back onto the same bearing as far as a 90° turn to the right. From here the way goes SW along the fence line – don't go through the gate – until eventually descending a few metres steeply to a very stony track. Turn right (W) and go uphill and through the next gate onto a smoother track. Counter-intuitively turn right, but for only a few metres to the junction with a tarred road.

A bit of a trudge follows, though through pleasant upland countryside, fields and forest typical of the Ardennes. Walk roughly S for 2km and then take the left fork in the road, still surfaced and heading increasingly SE and finally almost E. The exit from this road and the entrance to the forest is just after where the consistent leftward trend suddenly changes with a right-hand bend. Just ahead is a 'not GR' sign on a tree; the poorly signed path goes obliquely back into the trees. Initially it's almost parallel to the road – don't take the more obvious track at 90° to a road that ultimately peters out. Soon the path veers N and runs down to cross a major track just 250m after leaving the road. Directly opposite is the continuation, with no GR signs but a much wider path. After roughly 250m the path veers right and a deep

The Semois riverbank early in the route

valley becomes visible on the left. In a further 250m it rises to a viewpoint where there is a seat, a shelter and fine views of the Semois, the **Tombeau du Chevalier** and Herbeumont's fortress.

The route now follows the well-signed GR all the way to the main road. Start by leaving the viewpoint E and descend to cross a re-entrant before climbing up to the next viewpoint. After a further 200m go left at a fork, continuing gently downhill as far as a T-junction with a seat. Again turn left, still losing height, and continue to another T-junction and seat where you take another left

Herbeumont castle walls

turn. An excellent view of Herbeumont opens up 200m lower down, and just below this point there is another shelter. Ignoring a left fork, the GR now drops sharp right and narrows on its steep descent, emerging on the **N884** near a bridge over the Semois.

Turn right and walk for a few metres along the road before turning right onto a small road. Carry on up this until you can walk left onto the embankment of the **old railway line**. Turn back N and after 250m arrive on the viaduct, now used by walkers and cyclists.

From the south end of the viaduct it's just 1.3km back to the railway bridge below the car park, going through the old station and goods yard area (now a motorhome parking zone) and up the hill along Ave des Combattants, passing the tourist office, to the château **car park**. Don't forget the castle visit.

> **Herbeumont castle** sits on a rocky spur overlooking the village, high above the Semois. It was built in 1268 by Johan de Rochefort in a trapezoidal shape with corner towers and a keep in the gate area. The advent of artillery in the 16th century mandated a redesign that included thicker walls and the provision of ramparts large enough for cannon. It was dismantled sometime after 1657 on the orders of the French King Louis XIV. Entry is free; consider a picnic.

WALK 10
La Ramonette

Start/Finish	Pont de France in Bouillon
Distance	2km
Ascent	75m
Time	1hr
Map	Carte des promenades du Grand Bouillon (1:25,000)
Refreshments	Shops, cafés and restaurants in Bouillon
Access	To reach Bouillon by car, take the E411 (Brussels – Namur – Luxembourg) and come off at exit 25 onto the N89.

If you go to only one viewpoint this is the one to choose, situated on the small hill known as La Ramonette. At its lowest point it overlooks the castle very closely, and for this reason at one time there stood here a five-metre wooden tower, protected by earthworks and stockades, to protect the position.

From the Pont de France in Bouillon, go up the steep hill of the Vieille Route de France (the old high road to Sedan before the advent of the bypass). On the way pass an ornamental rock dedicated to the memory of poet Charles van Leberghe.

> **Charles van Lebergbe** (1861–1907), a well-known Flemish poet who wrote in French, is said to have written his famous poem *Le Chanson d'Ève* on that spot. Whether he was just sitting by the road when inspiration struck, or whether he had been toying with the idea for weeks when suddenly it all came together during this very walk, is something to ponder. *Chanson d'Ève* was his best-known work and was set to music by Gabriel Fauré.

A short distance further on there is an interesting *bac-abreuvoir* (watering point) for horses and goats, dating from 1773 and badly in need of restoration. Take the

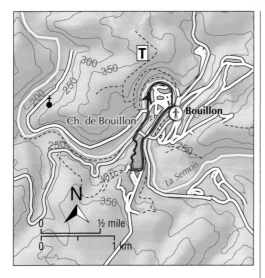

first turning right into Rue de l'Arboretum and follow it up to a T-junction; turn right and immediately right again

View from La Ramonette

onto a narrow surfaced lane, at the end of which take a grassy uphill path. There is a short climb to the top of La Ramonette, where there is a shelter.

Leave the top, going downhill towards the castle. On this path you find more views and seats, the best probably being the last when you are very close to the castle and can see a loop of river on both sides of it. Continuing down the path leads to the N810 Corbion road, just 250m from the road tunnel under the castle. Unless you have serious time pressures, walk back into **Bouillon** along the bow in the river and avoid the tunnel.

WALK 11

The Belvédère

Start/Finish	Pont de Liège in Bouillon
Distance	3.5km
Ascent	180m
Time	1hr30min
Map	Carte des promenades du Grand Bouillon (1:25,000)
Refreshments	Shops, cafés and restaurants in Bouillon
Access	To reach Bouillon by car, take the E411 (Brussels – Namur – Luxembourg) and come off at exit 25 onto the N89.

This 25m-high metallic structure can be seen on the skyline at a gap in the wooded hills to the north of the town. It is a large viewing platform and effectively sited for a panoramic view of the loop of the Semois that encloses Bouillon and its castle. After being closed for many years it reopened in 2012; however, it is unpredictably chained and locked. The walk up and down is a decent enough outing in its own right, so is included here in a spirit of optimism. For those of athletic persuasion this would make an excellent training run in dry conditions, although when wet it is very slippery.

Start at the Windsor Tea Room at the W end of the Pont de Liège in **Bouillon**. Walk down the west bank of the

Pont de Cordemois from Bouillon castle

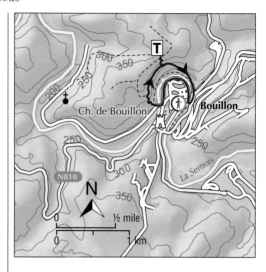

river, downstream, passing first under the Bastion du Dauphin and then the Bastion de Bretagne (defensive fortifications) before reaching the bridge known as the Pont de Cordemois (also known as 'Pont de Cordemoy' and 'Pont de Poulie'). Cross the river and go up steps, following GR signs and local path 15. Unremittingly steep zig-zags lead up through the woods before the gradient eases and the path contours NE. Ignore one small, unsigned path going acutely back to the left. Views of the town are fleeting when there are leaves on the trees, although in winter they're very grand. Keep left at a fork, still following GR signs, and go steeply again up to the **tower**.

The tower has two viewing platforms and, although there is a warning notice about not using it in snow or if you have a fear of heights, there are high walls for safety all the way up.

To return to the town retrace the ascent path down to the fork. Here go left and descend steeply to emerge on the Quai de la Tannerie, along which it's but a short step to the starting place in **Bouillon**.

WALK 12
Arboretum and patriots' memorial

Start/Finish	Pont de France in Bouillon
Distance	5km
Ascent	100m
Time	2hrs
Map	Carte des promenades du Grand Bouillon (1:25,000)
Refreshments	Shops, cafés and restaurants in Bouillon
Access	To reach Bouillon by car, take the E411 (Brussels – Namur – Luxembourg) and come off at exit 25 onto the N89.

An excellent outing for a short or evening walk in Bouillon and its immediate surroundings, educational and through varied countryside.

From the Pont de France in Bouillon, go up the steep hill of the Vieille Route de France (the old high road to Sedan), passing an ornamental rock dedicated to the memory of poet Charles van Leberghe, followed by a 1773 *bac-abreuvoir* (watering point) for horses and goats. Take the first turning right into Rue de l'Arboretum and follow it up to a T-junction.

Turn right and follow the road up as it curves left and back right again. Reach the entrance to the **arboretum** where there is a simple sign with a plan, and leave the road rightwards onto the nearest path. ▶ At the far end of the path there is another signboard and an option of turning down a level to see more trees; however, the current route goes directly ahead and takes the right fork some 50m on. After contouring around the head of a small re-entrant there are, when the trees are in leaf, glimpses of Bouillon and its castle before the path descends a spur and reaches a hairpin bend. Here on the left is a simple **memorial**, the Monuments des Fusillés, to three Belgian men shot there by the Gestapo in 1944.

The memorial alleges that the executions were ordered by **Leon Degrelle**, actually a native of

The trees are an exotic collection planted between 1906 and 1909 and examples are labelled throughout the area. A pair of binoculars to read the slightly more distant signs is distinctly advantageous.

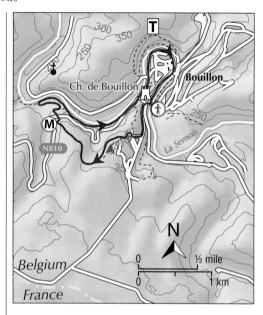

Bouillon, who joined the Waffen SS and later rose to command the Belgian contingent that became the 5th SS Volunteer Sturmbrigade Wallonien. In 1944 he had reached the rank of *Sturmbannfuhrer* (Major) and served on the eastern front. He survived the war and, although condemned to death in Belgium for treason, escaped to Spain where he was protected from extradition and where he died in 1994.

Drop down to the road and cross over to enter into the large Halliru camping and caravan site. Wind down towards the river, first on a tarred road and then using any likely paths. An eye for the best line is useful. Walk along the riverbank on a good path, passing a shrine to Notre Dame de Lourdes, after which the track is cobbled. Reach the N810 just 200m before the road tunnel under the castle and make your way back into **Bouillon** on the riverside or through the tunnel.

2 SPA

Biolètes Fagne (Walk 13)

The casino and the original baths in Spa

INTRODUCTION

Spa from the funicular railway

Spa seemed to us a charming little toyshop, surrounded by green hills and pleasant walks. It is just the place for invalids who love beautiful country as well as great comfort.
Katharine Macquoid,
In the Ardennes (1880)

Not many towns have gained the privilege of having their name incorporated into everyday language. Spa, French-speaking and the birthplace of Hercule Poirot, is a small town of some 10,000 inhabitants, situated about 40km southeast of Liège (and in the province of the same name) and 45km southwest of Aachen, lying in a valley and surrounded by wooded hills, mostly of beech and oak with a sprinkling of conifers. Famous for its healing cold springs and as a watering place since the 14th century, it has lent its name to any similar place that has springs claiming health-giving properties. The town amply demonstrates the long-standing popularity of thermal spas and the emergence of European tourism.

The first large-scale bathhouse, dating back to 1867 and now used for exhibitions, sits solidly on the south side of the Place Royale. Natural springs, locally known as *pouhons*, abound in the area. Tours are available to guide visitors around the town's springs, although it is rather more fun to pick up a booklet from the tourist office that is handily sited in the same building as the pouhon Pierre-le-Grand (Peter the Great visited the town to take the waters in 1718) and organize your own tour.

Although the phrase 'faded elegance' is sometimes used to describe this small town, it is actually quite a smart place with rather grand buildings, many dating from the 19th century. Spa suffered very little in the two world wars and in 1918 was the headquarters of the Imperial German army. The new thermal baths are situated on the Annette and Lubin hill, at the top of a funicular railway that runs up north from the Place Royale. It is a short but worthwhile and cheap excursion (€1 in 2012).

These days Spa is best known for the motor racing circuit at nearby Francorchamps and the town is jammed on race weekends, especially for F1 but also for classic car events. Check the dates before even trying to book a room.

Its proximity to the Hautes Fagnes country, one good example of which lies just a few kilometres south (Walk 14), means that it is a reasonable place to be based for exploration in that direction. For more information on the Hautes Fagnes, and for details of walks in that area, see Chapter 3.

ANNETTE AND LUBIN

The story of Annette and Lubin is very famous locally. They were, in reality, Gilles de Walt and Maria Schmitz, who lived from around 1750–1760 near the village of Nivezée (although some authorities have them as 'Joseph and Jeanne' and the parish records were destroyed in a fire in the 19th century). Their mothers, who were sisters, died leaving them orphaned from the age of about 14 and living under the same roof. They owned goats and sold the milk and local fruit to tourists, probably from a site close to the Tonnelet spring. At some stage they became lovers but as they were first cousins marriage was forbidden. Pregnancy ensued and with it the condemnation of the local church.

However, wealthy visitors pleaded special circumstances to Pope Benoît XIV and permission was granted to legalise the liaison, although there is no existing documentation supporting this. By 1764 the generosity of these benefactors included the provision of a small thatched dwelling, built on the Spaloumont plateau. By this time the couple had changed their names to Annette and Lubin, which were considered more attractive than their original names, in an attempt to improve their image. Subsequently the hill on which the new thermal baths is situated was named after them. Here they became a fashionable tourist attraction and sold meals, tea, coffee and beer. Indeed, by 1765 the Belgian composer Grétry had written a comic opera about them.

The story didn't end happily: financial problems ensued and in 1789 Lubin burned the house down to try and raise sympathy and thus money, but to no avail (at that time the French Revolution was a powerful distraction for visiting gentry). Ultimately Lubin became a hermit and lived in the forest until his death in 1799. The fates of Annette and the child are unknown.

WALK 13

Solwaster and the Statte stream

Start/Finish	Solwaster village car park
Distance	8.5km
Ascent	240m
Time	3hrs
Map	Pays des Sources carte nord: Spa –Theux – Jalhay (1:25,000)
Refreshments	Good café in Solwaster village
Access	Leave Spa eastwards on N629 via Balmoral and then turn right on the N640. Cross the motorway and turn left at the signpost for Solwaster village (11km).

This is probably the finest walk in the Spa area, combining a pretty woodland valley, an area of Fagne, local legends described on boards along the way, a nice village to start from and finish at and exemplary signage. The plan of the route allows a number of permutations. Children would love the first section up as far as the waterfall.

From the middle of Solwaster village walk along the road E, following blue rectangle signs. The road curves right and crosses the Statte stream; here turn right into

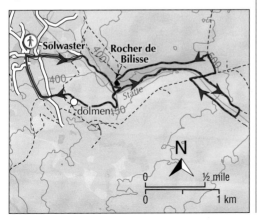

Typical bridge in the Statte valley

the woodland, the path following the stream closely with enough crossings, all on beautifully constructed bridges, to make your head spin.

The first obvious landmark is the **Rocher de Bilisse**, standing tall and vertical on the left of the path. There is an opportunity for a much closer inspection at a later stage of this walk. Continue upstream NE, taking care not to stray onto the path and stream that run south. The literally babbling brook is with you all the way to the next place of interest (the Cascade des Nutons – but don't expect too much there. As waterfalls go it ranks as minimalistic, but it's a nice place).

Nuton is an Ardenne word describing a special kind of gnome who lives in the forest and can be very mischievous. So on health and safety grounds beware.

The path now climbs up to the forest road, meeting it at a substantial bridge. Cross the bridge and turn left off the road to walk SE on a small path.

This is the very different country of the **Biolètes Fagne**. The oak and beech woodland of the first part of the walk has largely given way to birch and spruce, the planting of the latter on the Fagne being an intensive 19th-century development that significantly damaged the drainage and thus the peat bog. Attempts to remove the spruce are being made but it's a slow job.

The questionable dolmen

The brown, peat-coloured stream that runs alongside the path often contains whitish foam that is greasy to the touch. This is caused by **saponins** – unsaturated fatty acids that are naturally occurring and are not pollutants.

The path runs for 800m to an open area of Fagne that has been, to some extent, rehabilitated. Take a right turn at the signed junction. The route passes Le Pierrier (a stone field) and quickly leads to a forestry track. Turn right and walk back down to the road. Again go right here and cross the outward route, walking a further 300m to turn left on a surfaced road. However, just 200m on, turn left again at a large hut onto a track heading W and continue for just over 1km to a fork.

Take the left fork. The track soon swings left to emerge at the top of the Rocher de Bilisse with a bench and a view in a fine situation. The descent from here is steep but guarded by a sturdy handrail; at the bottom the sense of déjà vu continues as again you cross the outward track. Go downstream for 50m and then turn S over a bridge to climb up alongside a subsidiary stream. The height gain here is mercifully slight and the path bends right at the top to wander easily through the trees to the site of the **dolmen**.

This large, flat **block of quartzite** was apparently found by one Théodore Britte in 1887 when he was clearing waste ground. There has been much controversy about its origins but there is no clear evidence to support the local claim that it is actually a dolmen (a presumed burial chamber). Apart from not possessing the usual three or more upright supporting stones, there has been no demonstration of the existence of an underground chamber.

The last leg takes the route out of the forest and the second road on the right leads steadily down back into **Solwaster village**.

WALK 14
Fagne de Malchamps

Start/Finish	Place Royale in the centre of Spa
Distance	13km
Ascent	280m
Time	3hrs30min
Map	Pays des Sources carte nord: Spa –Theux – Jalhay (1:25,000)
Refreshments	All facilities in Spa
Access	Spa can be reached by car from Liège by taking the E25 and then the N697 southeast (40km).
Note	The blue diamond waymark for part of this route is worth noting, but sometimes it is too discreetly sited to be easily spotted.

Tear yourself away from the delights of Spa town and venture up into the oak and beech woods of the high ground to the south. The route includes a short section of walk in the Fagne de Malchamps, essential if you are not intending to do one of the bigger Fagne walks described in Chapter 3. As with the other walks starting in Spa, begin at the walking route signposts just between the old tourist office building and the cable railway in the Place Royale.

From the centre of Spa follow the N62 E in the direction of Francorchamps, going out past the Casino, Pouhon Pierre le Grand and, a little further on, the Cascade Monumentale which documents illustrious visitors to Spa, starting in the 16th century and finishing with most of the American generals of WWII and, finally, Baudouin I (King of Belgium until 1993) and his Queen Fabiola. About 700m from the start find the remains of a railway bridge and turn right into Rue Chelui. Cross the Square de la Resistance ahead, continuing on Rue Chelui for just 100m before turning right into Chemin de la Havette. Cross the small stream where the road bends left and follow the road to its end at the forest edge (1.8km from the start) where a path leads up to the right.

The surfaced road is soon forgotten as the path (blue triangles and, better, GR signs) climbs delightfully S through the beech and oak woods alongside La Picherotte, the small stream. Ignore the first two bridges and after 250m take the third. From here on there are

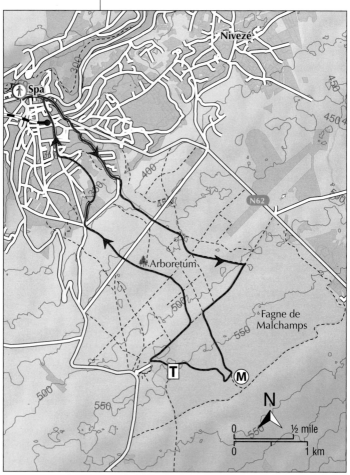

several bridges but the way is obvious and the markings good.

Cross a surfaced road and pick up another path immediately opposite (still GR signs) which leads to a spring (the Pouhon Delcor). In 2012 the water was non-potable – disappointing on a warm day. Shortly after the spring is a six-way junction; turn right along a main track (GR signs) and follow this for 300m to a five-way crossing where you turn left (ESE) onto a pleasant ride (leave the blue triangle signs here; GR signs continue).

La Picherotte

All this time it's been a steady climb and this continues a little further. At the T-junction at the top of the hill turn right onto another ride, wide and grassy, now with the beginnings of the Fagne country on the left and occasional glimpses of the slopes down towards Spa on the right. It's almost 1km along here to an information board and map where the route turns left onto a path that takes you onto the **Fagne de Malchamps** proper, leading SSE across this unusual and fascinating habitat to reach a **monument**.

Fagne de Malchamps Lancaster Bomber memorial

The **monument** commemorates the seven crew members of a Lancaster Bomber of 550 Squadron RAF, based at North Killingholme in Lincolnshire, shot down at 1.20am on 23 April 1944 by a Luftwaffe night fighter while returning from a bombing raid on Dusseldorf. The memorial is almost exactly on the site of the crash. The crew members were buried at the Commonwealth war cemetery at Heverlee, 3km south of Leuven.

This is the most southerly point of the walk. From the monument follow the raised boardwalk NW (still GR signs) across the open Fagne, passing information boards (French and Flemish) to reach a large **observation tower** (20m, climbable for the view). There is good cover and seating here if the weather is inclement.

> Just before the tower pass a cross, a tribute to **Dieudonne Jacobs** (1887–1967), an artist from Liège who specialized in painting scenes from the Hautes Fagnes and the Riviera where he lived.

This is the end of the boardwalk. Leave the tower and take the right fork in the track that leads down to a more complex junction by a large building. Turn right and after just 70m turn right again. It takes you back parallel to the Fagne for 700m to then turn left off the track downhill onto a tar road. Fortunately this doesn't last long. Go straight over the crossroads for 250m to reach the **arboretum** on the right. It's more pleasant to walk in the trees within the arboretum, parallel to the track, than on the track itself. There are labels on some trees but they are few and far between.

Leave the arboretum 300m further down onto the same road and continue down to the public road. Cross over onto a track and walk for 700m down to a five-way junction. Take the Route de la Géronstère for just a few paces before taking a path on the right that quickly becomes a delightful grassy lane. Be careful at the chicane (follow the blue diamond) and go down through woods to the outskirts of **Spa** where you turn right onto Route de la Géronstère.

This road leads directly downhill into town, passing Royal Spa FC's ground and the grand church of St Remacle.

WALK 15
Château de Franchimont

Start/Finish	Place Royale in the centre of Spa
Alternate finish	Franchimont station
Distance	7.5km outward; 9km return
Ascent	230m outward; 150m return
Time	2hrs30min outward; 3hrs return
Map	Pays des Sources carte nord: Spa –Theux – Jalhay (1:25,000)
Refreshments	All facilities in Spa; café just off-route in village of Theux
Access	Spa can be reached by car from Liège by taking the E25 and then the N697 southeast (40km).

A relatively easy walk to a very attractive historic castle with the bonus of a convenient, and optional, return train journey, combined with the choices of route, makes this a very flexible outing.

Begin at the walking route signposts in **Spa**, just between the old tourist office building and the cable railway in the Place Royale. The best way to start is to pay 1 per person and use this **funicular** to get up to the thermal baths complex on the hill north of town. For those who prefer to walk up, the path starts a few metres to the left of the funicular station and zig-zags all the way up to the spa complex.

If you can tear yourself away from the sybaritic delights within, walk up through the car park to the road. Turn left and go straight ahead across the roundabout and through the holiday complex known as Sol Cress. With the cemetery on your left, enter woodland just 250m from the start point and soon cross another track, following GR signs and a signpost for Sentier de l'Etang. Stick to the same track, soon winding right and downhill, to reach a T-junction in a valley. Turn left and after roughly 500m arrive at **L'Étang de Chawion** – a small tarn, which can be muddy and dull in wet weather but charming in better weather. There is a small shelter with seats at its north end.

Cross the N end of the tarn to its E side, go past a shed and walk N down the hill, going through a barrier and turning right where the main forestry track bends left. Here pick up green diamond signs that run from here all the way to the castle. Walk E along the track until it turns through almost 180° and heads up a spur with a shallow

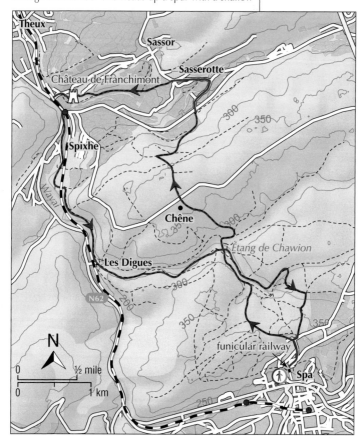

re-entrant on the right. There are a number of alternative tracks and paths but the way is well signed.

Towards the top of the hill pass the **Chêne de la Vierge Marie** (the Virgin Mary's oak, adorned with a small shrine), and cross over a main track at the highest point of the walk. Continue roughly N, soon downhill and still well signed, until after veering NW you see open land a little way ahead. Here there is a sharp rightward turn downhill to a track crossroads by an ancient oak. Go straight across and steeply down to end up joining another track at the side of a field. After turning N again you arrive at a main road.

Cross over into a surfaced lane and follow this to a left turn over a stream. The lane leads uphill and NW. Turn left into the highly attractive, tiny hamlet of **Sasserotte**, now joining a GR. A few metres down into the hamlet look carefully right for the onward path tucked in between two houses. This narrow path winds through a band of trees and shrubs to emerge on open land. Keep left and go down to a kissing gate, diagonally across the next field to the next gate and then along the

Étang de Chawion

Château de Franchimont

right side of a long narrow field, looking out for the exit through yet another gate. From here the path leads along and down before branching right at a fork which leads up to the **castle** entrance.

> **Château de Franchimont** was probably built in the 11th century and extended several times, notably in the 16th century when the outer wall was added. It is still possible to descend, with great care, the very steep staircase that leads down between the outer walls into the casemates (vaulted chambers built to contain cannon).
>
> The tour starts with a film and a small exhibition; an English version audio guide is available, the entrance fee is cheap and the whole thing is both highly recommendable and really good value.

When leaving the castle go round the walls clockwise. This path winds down through woods to a school; keep right for a few metres then turn left and cross the railway. Go up to the main road, turn left, and walk 250m to where you can turn left and either cross the railway to get onto the station platform or turn right immediately before the level crossing to return to Spa on foot.

> **Franchimont station** has trains every hour for Spa. It is not necessary to have a ticket to board the train but you must alert the guard to your presence and ask to buy a ticket or a penalty may be levied. So shout something to him – almost anything in any language will do, provided you include the word 'ticket' – so that you can claim he was notified.

If you are not taking the train, keep the railway to your left and go down the small path by the river **Wayai**. Just upstream is the eastern part of the village of **Spixhe**. Do not cross the bridge to the right but continue ahead on a tarred road that soon becomes unsurfaced and turns sharply left to cross the railway. On the other side of the tracks turn right and continue along this undulating path to reach a tiny place called **Les Digues**. Be sure to cross the stream and then turn left, thereby keeping the stream on your left. Walk uphill on this track for a little over 2km and reach **L'Étang de Chawion**, completing a circuit.

Here there is a choice. One possibility is simply to reverse the outward route (about 2km and 80m ascent); the other is to make the walk into a figure-of-eight pattern. For the latter, cross the dam wall at the north end of the tarn, going past the hut and up onto the track beyond (the attractively named Avenue Princesse Clémentine). Turn right and walk uphill, going around a dramatic, almost 180°, bend to the right, as far as a crossroads of paths at a field corner. Turn right (signposted Spaloumont and Spa) and after a short descent to cross a brook, climb up the other side to reach a road by the Sol Cress holiday complex. Go downhill and turn left to go back to the car park by the thermal bath complex (2.8km; 80m ascent).

Whichever option you choose, if you decide to walk down to the town go into the cul-de-sac to the left of the buildings and keep right until the obvious descent path appears. It's about 500m down to the start point of the outing in Spa.

WALK 16

L'Étang de Chawion and Lac de Warfaaz

Start/Finish	Place Royale in the centre of Spa
Distance	9.5km
Ascent	180m
Time	3hrs
Map	Pays des Sources carte nord: Spa –Theux – Jalhay (1:25,000)
Refreshments	All facilities in Spa; food and drink available to buy at Lac de Warfaaz (unreliable out of high season)
Access	Spa can be reached by car from Liège by taking the E25 and then the N697 southeast (40km).

This walk explores the forest to the north of Spa, taking in a tarn and a more substantial (although still small) lake, with little height gain and modest distance.

Parc de Sept Heures, created in 1758, at the start of the walk

WALKING IN THE ARDENNES

Begin at the walking route signposts in **Spa** between the old tourist office building and the cable railway in the Place Royale. Consider using the **funicular** (€1) to get up to the thermal baths complex on the hill north of town. (For those who prefer to walk up, the path starts a few metres to the left of the funicular station and zig-zags all the way up to the spa complex.) From there, walk up through the car park to the road. Turn left and go straight ahead across the roundabout and through the Sol Cress holiday complex. With the cemetery on your left, enter woodland just 250m from the start point and soon cross another track, following GR signs and a signpost for Sentier de l'Etang. Stick to the same track, soon winding right and downhill, to reach a T-junction in a valley. Turn left and after roughly 500m arrive at **L'Étang de Chawion**. There is a small shelter with seats at its north end.

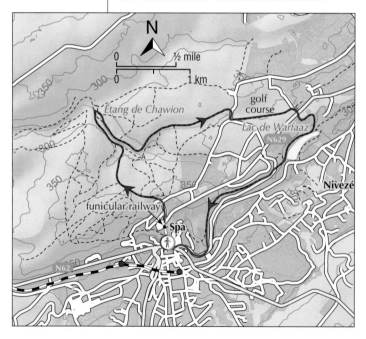

Lac de Warfaaz

Go down from the path to the shelter; cross over to the E side past the hut and go up to the Avenue Princesse Clémentine. Turn right and walk uphill to the point where this track makes a dramatic, almost 180°, bend to the right. **Don't go round this bend**. Instead go straight ahead on a smaller path with a tiny stream (almost a ditch), the Ruisseau du Petit Chawion, close by on the right. Don't cross the bridge on the right after about 300m but continue straight on. The path rises gently as far as a surfaced road.

Turn right and after 100m, immediately before the road junction, turn left onto a broad track through the trees at the edge of a field, later the **golf course**. After almost 1km this track ends, also on a tarred road. Turn right down to the main road and go diagonally left across it to a small lane signposted Sentier de la Fourche. There are two sharp bends, left then right, as this path drops down into a valley. Another small path joins from the left, but look out for the next (unsigned) path left that leads ahead and down to deposit you at the water's edge near the northeast end of the **Lac de Warfaaz**.

> The most pleasant little **Lac de Warfaaz** is not a natural phenomenon; it was constructed in 1892 by damming the river Wayai that originates up on the Hautes Fagnes. The lakeside path has benches to rest on, fishermen to watch, large numbers of mallard to feed but, most importantly, establishments offering food or drink or both, albeit open only in high season and irregularly at other times.

Walk for 500m SW along the lakeside path. Just before you join the road a small path climbs steeply up the hill (GR markings) and goes up to the main road. Cross the road to the obvious continuation and, following a blue/white/blue trail sign, walk back to town. Don't be seduced by other path options, although it is acceptable to consider seduction by the very grand houses and land above.

You arrive in **Spa** by the Carrefour supermarket. Continuing down the road brings you past the tourist office (in the Pouhon Pierre-le-Grand) and, turning right, quickly back to the Place Royale.

3 HAUTES FAGNES, MALMEDY AND STAVELOT

Typical scene on the boardwalk crossing the Hautes Fagnes (Walk 17)

INTRODUCTION

THE HAUTES FAGNES

The first known written reference to the Hautes Fagnes (*Hohes Venn* in German) dates from the end of the seventh century. The name probably has origins in the Proto-Germanic *fanja* and Old Frisian *fenne*. The old English word *fenn* has the same root.

The Hautes Fagnes National Nature Reserve was created in 1957, extending from Eupen in the north to Monschau in the east, almost to Spa in the west and close to Malmedy in the south. It features the highest point in Belgium, the Signal de Botrange (694m) – until 1999 a meteorological station but now a restaurant café and a telecoms tower. Today it forms part of the much larger 'Parc Naturel Hautes Fagnes – Eifel', having merged with the German Eifel park. Some sections, clearly marked on walking maps, are open only to guided parties or are completely closed, but much is available to all. You must stay on the roads, tracks, paths and walkways, indeed the *caillebotis* (boardwalks) are one of the great attractions of the area.

Originally this was a wooded area with oak, beech, silver birch, hazel and alder predominating. Human intervention – notably wood clearance, over-grazing, peat extraction and the creation of multiple ditches associated with spruce planting – has dramatically changed the landscape, but there is considerable ongoing effort to reverse these effects. What remains today is a mixture of peat bog, fenland, dry moorland, semi-natural grassland and the dreaded spruce plantations.

Although peat bogs are the best known of these habitats they constitute less than three per cent of the total area. Here the extremely wet climate and minimally permeable sub-soil leads to stagnant water that is poorly oxygenated, acidic and low in minerals. In turn this encourages the establishment of sphagnum mosses and sedge and does not support fish, plants and flowers. Organic matter (dead plants, for example) scarcely decomposes but accumulates as peat.

The fenland has mineral-rich surface water, the original source of the Spa springs. This water is neutral or alkaline and, unlike the peat bogs, supports a variety of plants and fish.

The dry moorland is largely where beech woods originally stood on gentle slopes and permeable soil. Here, heather, bilberry and low shrubs predominate. Some effort is put into maintaining the semi-natural grassland as a move to biodiversity, even though it was not part of the original ecosystem. Some grass-cutting takes place and there is an attempt to reintroduce limited and controlled grazing.

The spruce plantations, never part of the original Fagnes, were introduced in the 19th century and the systematic drainage associated with it has been very harmful to the other original habitats, notably peat bogs. Gradually they are being removed.

The Fagnes is a botanist's paradise, not so much for the number of species but for the unusual variety.

MALMEDY

This small town lies in a wooded valley at the confluence of the rivers Warche and Warchesse. In truth it has little to commend it as a holiday destination in itself, indeed entering from the west is particularly unprepossessing, but it's pleasant enough and handily placed for the Hautes Fagnes.

Although in older sources the town name is spelled with an accent (Malmédy), the current official spelling is as above. Politically it lies in the province of Liège and region of Wallonia, although some 20 per cent of the inhabitants speak German as their native language.

In December 1944 it was severely damaged by Allied bombing with significant loss of life to the civilian population. Sadly, it is best known among many tourists and military historians for the murder of American prisoners by some members of the German army at Baugnez crossroads.

THE INCIDENT AT BAUGNEZ CROSSROADS, 17 DECEMBER 1944

Kampfgruppe Peiper, commanded by Obersturmbannfuhrer (Lt Colonel) Joachim Peiper, was part of the 1st SS Panzer Division that, in Operation Herbstnebel, had orders to move via Ligneuville to Stavelot, Trois Ponts and eventually to Huy to capture and hold the Meuse bridges in that area. Peiper was the model for the character Colonel Hessler (played by Robert Shaw) in the 1965 film *The Battle of the Bulge*.

Because of the poor state of his intended route from Thirimont to Ligneuville, Peiper made a diversion via the Baugnez crossroads near Malmedy. Here his leading tanks surprised a unit of the US 285th Field Artillery Observation Battalion, who dismounted and surrendered. Exactly what happened next and why is unclear to this day, but ultimately a large number of the prisoners, probably more than 80, were shot dead by some of the SS troops.

Soldiers of this unit were implicated in similar incidents, not just involving US prisoners but also a particularly savage killing of civilians in Stavelot a few days later. Regrettably, both sides executed prisoners in this short campaign but 1st SS Panzer Division particularly were implicated.

There is a memorial at the crossroads on the opposite side of the road to the field where the killings took place, and a small museum nearby.

WALK 17

An excursion in the Hautes Fagnes

Start/Finish	Baraque Michel
Distance	13.5km
Ascent	120m
Time	4hrs30min
Map	Haute Fagnes Carte des promenades (1:25,000)
Refreshments	No facilities
Access	Baraque Michel lies 14km north of Malmedy on N68. Parking adjacent.

This walk is a good taster of what the real Hautes Fagnes offers. There is an extensive network of marked paths through mixed terrain with a large number of spruce, widespread willow and birch, some beech, oak and alder and, of course, fens, streams and the active peat bogs. The most impressive feature is the large open areas of wetland seen from one of the several boardwalks. Pick your day to visit; on an average of 176 days per year it is very misty and on 170 days per year it rains. But it's truly well worth it.

> **Baraque Michel** was an old hostel for travellers and traders, dating from the early 19th century and founded by Michel Schmitz, originally a tailor from the nearby village of Herbiester.

Start the walk at the **chapel** that stands alongside the baraque.

> **Fischbach chapel** was founded by Henri-Toussaint Fischbach, a Malmedy industrialist, as a gesture to the Almighty for the saving of his father-in-law, lost on the Fagne, by innkeepers from Baraque Michel. He established the principle that thereafter the innkeepers should ring a bell at the inn and light a lantern at the top of the chapel each night to guide travellers who might be lost. This was discontinued when the new Eupen to Malmedy road was constructed in 1856.

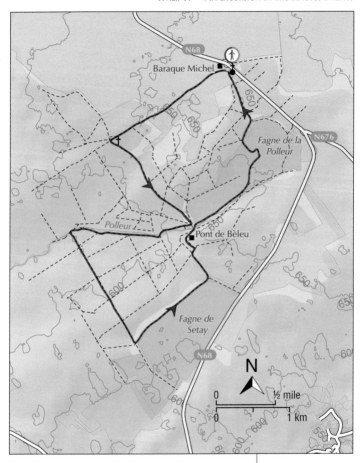

Initially the route follows the local path marked by a green rectangle and sets off SW on a boardwalk. Although this finishes after about 1.2km, stretches of boards recur from time to time at especially boggy places. If they are slippery it makes for somewhat uneasy progress.

After 700m, now in fairly open woodland, there is an old marker stone for the path with an adjacent **cross**.

Croix des Fiancés

The **Croix des Fiancés** commemorates the demise of François Reiff and Marie-Josephe Solherd, an engaged couple who died in January 1871 in the snow while attempting to cross east-to-west to reach the village of Xhoffraix. They had been warned against the journey when they stopped in a coffee shop in Jalhay because they had inappropriate clothing and no provisions.

Shortly after this sad place of commemoration, turn left at the junction and continue on the path until, rather unexpectedly, you hit a tar road. This is an important landmark – if a shorter outing is required, go downhill for 150m to the bridge (**Pont de Bèleu**) and pick up the return route.

For the normal route go SE down the surfaced road for just 50m and then turn right onto a small path that soon picks up the **Polleur** stream. After wet weather this section is very muddy and slow. Slow, because most people prefer not to go in over the ankles and instead expend considerable energy performing agile manoeuvres to avoid so doing. The little path winds among small trees, crosses the stream and emerges on a broad forestry track. The map is a little misleading here but you should follow the broad track right (NW), the stream just on your right.

About 400m on, the signs take you down a small path to the right. This is the purist's way and is very pretty, running close to the stream again, meeting another path and turning quite abruptly left to arrive at a crossroads. Ignoring this small path cuts off a corner and leads to the same crossroads.

From the crossroads go straight on (SE) for almost 2km, crossing GR573 (where you leave the green rectangular signs, although you meet them again later) and continuing to reach another open area, the **Fagne de Setay**.

Now turn left and walk a delightful 1.5km between woodland and fen. At the T-junction turn left and reach the tar road again. Right and then left turns lead to the small-roofed refuge at **Pont de Bèleu**.

A well-prepared path with descriptive signboards, part of an educational journey across the Fagne de la Polleur, leads rightwards. After 1km reach the **Fagne de la Polleur** itself and the path that circumnavigates it.

Back over the Fagne de la Polleur

Convention dictates that you walk clockwise, so keep left at the signboard where the boardwalk starts again. Another impressive open area of Fagne beckons with, in the spring, meadow pipits by the dozen doing their impressive parachute displays.

At the end of the boards, at another display panel and map, be careful to take the track left (NW) and avoid another circuit of the Fagne. This quickly leads back to the **Baraque Michel** in about 750m.

WALK 18
Kaiser Karl's Bettstatt

Start/Finish	Nahtsief parking area
Distance	17km
Ascent	170m
Time	4hrs30min
Map	Haute Fagnes Carte des promenades (1:25,000)
Refreshments	No facilities
Access	Nahtsief is 12km southeast of Eupen on the N67, just over 1km west of the German frontier at Mützenich.
Note	This otherwise excellent route is mildly impaired by two sections of surfaced, though narrow, lane-walking (1.5km and 1km respectively), but these are both in the nature reserve and carry only official vehicles and cyclists.

This is a tour of the more northern section of the Hautes Fagnes, known locally in its German form, *Hohes Venn*. The scenery from the boardwalks is rather different than that of Walk 17, being more closed in by smaller bushes and trees. Given the serious events of 20th-century history hereabouts, it seems odd to be able to traverse the Belgium-Germany frontier at will. Look out for Kaiser Karl's special place on the way round.

From the **N67** parking area walk N into the nature reserve for 150m and then take the small, unsigned boardwalk on the right. Early on the path is grassy or muddy, but it soon becomes boarded and passes through clumps of dwarfed silver birches, heathland and bog. At about 1km the boardwalk divides; go right and continue E through similar terrain for 1km to a second junction. Take the left option, signposted Kaiser Karl's Bettstatt.

600m later the boardwalk comes to an end. Turn right onto a grassy ride and immediately keep left past or under a barrier, following the short ride to its end to find and continue along a very small path. This leads generally NE. After a path joins from the right at border stone 721, **Kaiser Karl's Bettstatt**, the alleged sleeping place

KAISER KARL'S BETTSTATT

Essentially this is one of two large quartzite rocks in the unlikely situation of an otherwise rock-free woodland. Legend has it that Kaiser Karl (aka Charles I of Austria and Charles IV of Hungary, the last ruler of the Austro-Hungarian Empire from 1916 to 1918) was hunting in the forest and some distance from the court at Konzen, between Aachen and Monschau. Night fell and the party elected to stay in the forest. The large rock seemed a bed fit for an emperor and down he lay.

So far, just about believable. But possibly a legendary leap too far is that his servant, the night being cold, offered Karl the use of his cap. Karl declined, using the 'low German' words *"Mütze nich"* (no hat). This, the story relates, is why the local village is called Mützenich.

Interestingly, some authors refer to the stones as *Le lit de Charlemagne* (the bed of Charles the Great, who died in nearby Aachen in AD814) so, although a great story, the whole idea should be taken with a considerable pinch of salt.

of Kaiser Karl Franz Joseph Ludwig Hubert Georg Otto Marie von Hapsburg-Lothringen, lies just ahead.

Leaving the king's resting place, just ahead is a shelter. Keep left and follow the forest edge for about 900m to a place called Steling – just an open grassy area with a weather station. Continue in the same direction, roughly

One of the numbered stones marking the border between Belgium and Germany

NE, for 2.5km along a good forest track through mixed woodland, noting the border stones which give the clue when you veer away from the German frontier.

> Two thirds of the way along this section of the route look out for the *Roderkreuz* – a **way-side cross** in memorial to one Alois Roder of Mützenich, a 36-year-old smuggler who was shot dead by a customs officer in July 1935 when he declined to comply with an instruction to halt. How times change.

Roderkreuz: a wayside memorial to Alois Roder

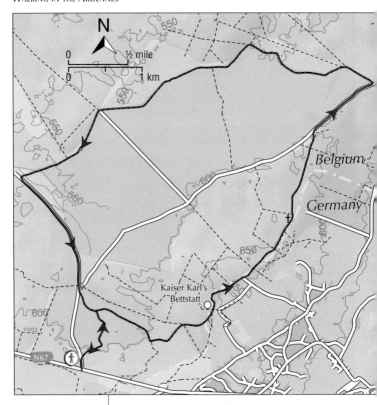

The path turns sharply left and joins a tarred forest road. Walk rightwards along the road for 1200m to a junction with lots of signs and a bench. Turn left here and pass a nature trail with, a little further on, a children's play area at a path junction. Turn left again and within 60m lies the entrance to another boardwalk, this time almost 1.5km in length. It is slightly shorter to use the path along the forest edge, but this rather defeats the purpose of the walk.

At the end of the boardwalk turn left (SW) along a lovely grass track that is soft, almost spongy underfoot,

The pretty Entenpfuhl

with evidence of historic peat extraction. Cross a surfaced road and continue SW, grassy again with occasional boarded sections, to finish through woodland,
crossing a more substantial **stream** than you have hitherto
encountered and reaching another surfaced road.

Unless the walking distance is to attain epic propor-
tions there is no alternative now to turning left and trudging down the tar, albeit through peaceful and pleasant
surroundings. However, at the next crossroads turn left
for 40m and then right onto the boardwalk again by the
Entenpfuhl (literally 'duck pond'). This path meets the
outward march at the first junction (so turn right) but is
a more interesting, if marginally longer, way to return to
the **N67** car park than simply continuing down the road.

WALK 19

Cascade and canyon

Start/Finish	Auberge du Moulin de Bayhon
Distance	10km
Ascent	200m
Time	3hrs30min
Map	Haute Fagnes Carte des Promenades (1:25,000) or Au Pied des Fagnes Carte des Promenades (1:25,000)
Refreshments	No facilities
Access	Drive from Malmedy to Robertville, then to Ovifat. Continue west until, after negotiating a couple of hairpin bends, you reach a bridge at the start. Limited parking.

This outing provides a superb round trip on good paths from a deep, wooded valley to touch the Fagne before heading back down again. A waterfall, narrow, deep river valleys and dozens of picnic places entertain en route. It is described in more detail than usual as the currently available map is difficult to follow, overprinting much topographic detail with thick lines representing paths.

Start by going N down the track on the right of the Bayehon stream (the name is spelled differently in different sources) and soon cross on a bridge or by the ford. This choice of crossing is a recurring theme of the walk. Soon cross back right and, where the stream bends left, note a path (GR) joining from a small valley on the right. Continue easily and pleasantly along the main stream, now walking NW. Pass a bridge and a wooden signpost for **Longfaye village** and 600m after this re-cross the river. Keeping right at the next fork (follow GR signs) leads up to a seat perched just above the well-known **waterfall**, Cascade du Bayhon. This section of the walk is very popular in summer. It's a very small waterfall but a pleasant place for a break. If the weather is inclement, go a few metres up the path to the T-junction, turn right and just down the slope you'll find a good **shelter**.

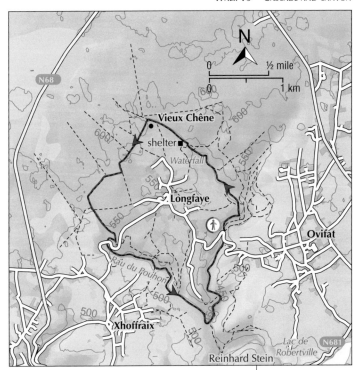

From the shelter follow the signpost Botrange and Vieux Chêne. Keep close to the steam over awkward tree roots and pass the actual **Vieux Chêne** (old oak) that stands to the left of the path. Go straight across the next crossing (the path for Longfaye goes left) and continue 125m to turn left (SW). This is the most northerly point on the walk.

Although the ride and more open ground is inviting, if the ground is boggy after rain there is easier walking just inside the wood. Cross the highest point of the walk, almost 610m, and reach a track crossing. Go straight ahead and follow the track round to the left to find a small path going right (with a signpost). This path

Cascade du Bayhon

gradually turns S to reach another track crossing and continues ahead SE, going downhill towards the Longfaye road. Be careful here: the main track can lead you falsely left. The true way darts off to the right to reach the road a crucial few metres SW.

Cross the road diagonally right to find an excellent path settling down to run SE with the **Rau du Pouhon** stream just below. (If you are not following a stream then you are on the wrong path and are too far north.) Follow this down for almost 3km, ignoring other options until reaching the confluence with the Bayehon stream. It's a delightful descent, always by the river, the valley becoming very deep and wooded and the sides steeper. The use of the word 'canyon' locally is only a slight exaggeration.

The meeting of the two streams is a nice place with a seat. Turn N here, upstream. Cross the stream by bridge or ford three times and in 2km of gentle uphill walking reach the old mill and the parking area.

WALK 20
Château de Reinhardstein

Start/Finish	Car park on the south side of the Robertville dam
Distance	6.5km
Ascent	220m
Time	2hrs30min
Map	Haute Fagnes Carte des Promenades (1:25,000) or Au Pied des Fagnes Carte des Promenades (1:25,000)
Refreshments	No facilities
Access	From Malmedy take the N681 northeast for about 7km to the hamlet of Walk. Continuing on the same road north reaches the car park at the dam after about 750m.

A thoroughly enjoyable circular woodland walk with tumbling streams and an extraordinary 14th-century castle reconstructed using original plans.

The path leaves from the rear left-hand corner of the parking area at the **dam** and has green rectangles as a waymark throughout. It's a fine beginning, the path curving around the top of a conifer plantation with a steep drop

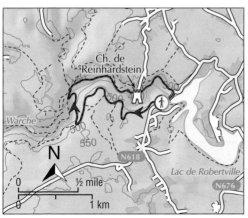

on the right, the lovely restored castle appearing through the trees across the valley. There is a closer view from the other side on the return leg near to the entrance to the castle.

> The **Château de Reinhardstein** was originally constructed in 1354, although there were some buildings on the site before that. It fell into ruin and was only rebuilt to its current very fine, almost fairytale, condition in 1969. Although it is still inhabited, visits are possible.

Château de Reinhardstein

There is a sharp descent into the valley but before reaching the floor a path junction offers an escape up to the left, the signpost nearby adding 'Napoleon's nose' to the itinerary. This turns out to be a rocky promontory near to the crest of the hill with a decent view of the uplands in the vicinity of the village of Xhoffraix (drop the 'X' when pronouncing). On the climb up keep in the woods when you touch some farmland and ignore a path on the right to the cascades – unless you decide to visit them as an extra. They are not world-beaters.

The descent into the Warche valley is easy, S and then SW, to arrive at a path junction. Turn back right (NE) and note that the accompanying GR goes the other way. At the bottom of the hill the river tumbles along attractively with lots of options for a waterside dalliance. Cross by walking 80m downstream to the bridge and then back up the other bank to cross the Bayehon stream, just above the confluence with the **Warche** that has run down from the Lac de Robertville dam.

The first section of the return walk back to the dam and the car park is fairly flat and runs alongside the delightful river. At the riverside track junction **don't** go down towards the river and **don't** go acutely back up left. Rather, take the middle option that goes steeply up in zig-zags to meet a larger path. Turn right and continue the climb. At the crest of the rise suddenly the **château** is close by. A few metres further on cross its drive, cross the stream bridge to the other side and continue up and back to the **dam**. There are some lateral tracks to tempt the unwary but the signing is good.

WALK 21

Stavelot, Coo and Trois Ponts triangle

Start/Finish	At the abbey in the centre of Stavelot
Distance	22.5km
Ascent	600m
Time	7hrs30min
Map	Pays de Stavelot (Coo–Francorchamps–Hockai) 1:25,000
Refreshments	Lots of facilities in all three places
Access	Stavelot is 8km southwest by road from Malmedy on the N68.

The three focal points of this walk are linked not only by the Amblève river but inevitably by the events of December 1944. This walk is a neat way of connecting them, and of seeing much of the surrounding countryside on the way.

An old abbey seems an ideal place to start a walk, and so it is with this walk from **Stavelot**. Leave W from the front of the ruins along the cobbled Rue Henri Massange that soon becomes Rue Neuve. Pass the Ferdinand Nicolay fountain and, at the top of the road, cross over the roundabout into Ave André Grégoire. Turn right at the top and go up to cross the RAVeL cycle track, keeping left into Chemin de Parfondruy.

As the road goes up the hill the houses are further apart, larger and more affluent. Keep left at a fork and avoid the road to Ster. Just after the last house on the right there is a track; originally this climbed the slope through woodland but recent felling has made it a much more open area. Follow the track, the broad valley of the Amblève on the left, until it meets a surfaced road. Go left for just a few paces and then take another track to the right. Just over 100m up here, turn sharp right (N) and walk along the edge of the woodland (forestry work may change this in the near future). At the highest point there is a convenient and roofed picnic table.

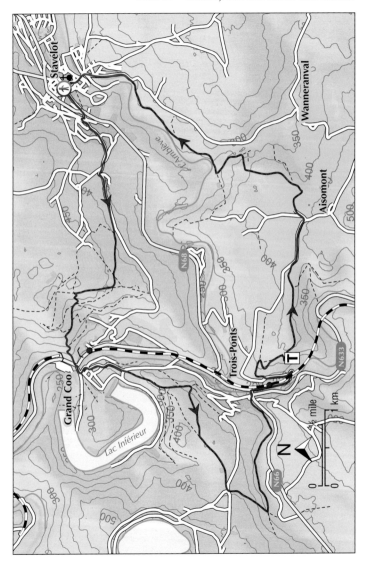

COO

"Perhaps," she said complacently, "we also shall have a station at Coo."
A station at Coo! The idea of an engine hissing and snorting in the quiet
peaceful valley was profanation; but naturally our placid, dark-eyed friend
was thinking of her pocket rather than the ruin which a station must bring to
the special charm of Coo.

Katharine Macquoid, describing a conversation with the owner
of the Hotel de la Cascade at Coo *(In the Ardennes*, 1880)

The Coo Falls have been famous as a tourist attraction for 150 years. At 15m in height they are hailed by some as the highest in Belgium. The smaller, right-hand fall, when seen from below, was the original and some sources say that the larger fall was cut by monks from Stavelot Abbey in the 18th century to protect Petit Coo (the upper village) from flooding. The latter is now a very touristy village, consisting mostly of eating establishments. The lower village holds 'Plopsa Coo', an entertainment park undeniably popular with families but hardly enhancing rural tranquility (visitors like the Macquoids would now find Coo unrecognizable and probably unacceptable) and there is also a station.

There is a nice little walk, not described here, from Grand Coo down the Amblève and, after crossing a bridge, up the hill to the pleasant village of La Gleize with its important WWII military history, a museum to describe it and, to complete the scene, a Panther tank parked outside.

Just after this the route goes down to the left, a delightful path through deciduous woodland, following GR signs. They lead down the hillside to a flight of steps spilling you onto the main road (N633) a few metres N of the way into **Grand Coo**.

Turn left down the road for the short walk down to the bridge that crosses the Coo falls. Leave the bridge over the cascades into Petit Coo, turning right in front of the Val de la Cascade restaurant and then left into Sur les Fosses. The surfaced road climbs gradually to the edge of a wood.

It is possible to save over 3km in distance and over 150m climb by continuing along the road from this point, staying on the same side of the river to avoid the main road. This takes an infinitely less interesting but much more direct line to Trois Ponts.

A track, which includes the red/white signs of a GR, leads into the wood and up the obvious spur. Keep left at the first and second forks to arrive at a third fork by a

Croix des Chênes

bench. Keep left again, following GR signs, going slightly
downhill with a nice vista of the wooded hills on the east
bank of the river. Some 400m from the last junction and
just after a bend in the track, take a path on the right up
into deciduous woodland (GR signs). This goes uphill to
emerge in open ground at a seat.

Continue SW alongside the wood, passing an
unsightly electricity station, to reach a road. Walk right
for 70m to the Croix des Chênes that is exactly what it
purports to be – a cross pitched between two oaks. Leave
the GR here and go left and downhill on a good track. In
the valley below turn left back towards Trois Ponts, following the Bodeux stream for about 2km until crossing
it via a choice of ford or wooden bridge. It is then but a
short step to arrive at the N66 as it runs down to a 90°
left-hand bend at the bottom of the gentle hill. At the corner turn right and go uphill to the now unstaffed **Trois
Ponts** railway station with its original cobbled platform
(trains for Luxembourg and Liège).

> **Trois Ponts** has had a railway station since the
> 1870s; this was from where the Macquoid fam-
> ily walked to Coo. However, the small town only
> reached immortality in December 1944 when US
> soldiers managed to demolish both the significant
> bridges and delay the thrust of Kampfgruppe Peiper.

Leave the station uphill and cross over the railway
bridge. The road curves in a hairpin and passes the oddly
named Belvédère Hallet – odd because it has no view
whatsoever. Now follow GR signs, leaving the road to
go right and up into an oak wood. Higher up there is a
counter-intuitive turn right onto a track but it leads you
true up to a real **viewpoint**, Le Tour Leroux, with decent
views from the top and, importantly, good seating.

The track with its GR signs joins a local road higher
up and soon arrives in the hamlet of **Aisomont**. Leave the
GR temporarily, turn left and then fork immediately right,
past some houses to find a path going downhill bending E. Further down the hill go through a dark conifer

wood (possibly soon to be felled) and zig-zag down to the stream in the valley at Croix de Remiheid (which has no visible cross). Don't cross the stream but turn left and take this narrow path to coast down to a path junction where you pick up the GR again.

Turn acutely right and go down the path leading to a potentially wet crossing of the Bouvin stream just before its confluence with the **Amblève**. All that remains is to continue along this path NE, climbing to cross a shoulder but otherwise easily, up to a road junction. This road leads speedily to the river bridge at **Stavelot**, guarded by a WWII US half-track. Cross the river and the abbey is just ahead.

Stavelot Abbey – only the west door remains in a freestanding tower

STAVELOT

Many people consider Stavelot to be the most attractive town on the Amblève river, set as it is in a pleasant shallow valley, with a number of half-timbered 18th-century houses and narrow lanes leading out from the cobbled and central Place St Remacle. In addition it has a particularly interesting historical canvas.

Almost on the banks of the Amblève river, the first Stavelot abbey was founded in the seventh century by St Remaclus (or Remacle), a Benedictine missionary bishop. A completely new abbey church was built in the 11th century. The 17th century saw a succession of terrible wars completely destroy both Stavelot and Malmedy, but the abbey and its church survived, only to be devastated during the French Revolution. What you see now are the remains of the freestanding tower that contained the west door and the recently enhanced footprint of the foundations of the rest of the church.

The town's coat of arms was granted in 1819. Its upper half consists of the 17th-century seal of the Prince-Abbot of Stavelot and its lower portion features a wolf with panniers on its back. The wolf is a recurring theme ▶

throughout Stavelot (look out for it on Walk 21 at the Ferdinand Nicolay fountain); the story is that when St Remaclus was originally constructing his place of worship he had but a donkey to help. When a wolf killed the donkey, transport of building materials became problematical. Fortunately, such were the powers of persuasion of the good priest that the wolf renounced his evil ways and, equipped with panniers across his back, carried stones to the building site.

Renovations from 1999 to 2002 rebuilt the cloister on old foundations and the abbey now incorporates three museums – the town museum, the Francorchamps racing circuit museum and that relating to the poet Guillaume Apollinaire – as well as the tourist office.

The 'blanc moussis'

The famous Stavelot Bible, created between 1093 and 1097 and currently in the British Museum, was produced by at least two Benedictine monks (brothers Ernesto and Goderannus), probably, but not certainly, within the abbey. It was completed 'when Jerusalem was under attack by many peoples', presumably the first crusade.

Any description of Stavelot is incomplete without mention of the extraordinary event, held annually on the third Sunday before Easter (the fourth Sunday of Lent), called *Laetare*, the catholic religious word for that particular day. It is a grandiose carnival with about 15 differently dressed groups taking part. The most famous are the '*blancs moussis*', dressed the same every year, whose images appear throughout the town year-round. Their white gowns and large red noses are both amusing and eerily reminiscent of the film *Scream*, although any hint of menace is speedily dispelled by their habit of throwing confetti and hitting bystanders with a dried pig's bladder. Although Laetare has its origins in the 16th century it's been a regular event since 1820. Accommodation is booked a year in advance so don't rely on just turning up to experience the fun.

4 DINANT, THE MEUSE AND THE LESSE

Roches de Freÿr (Walk 22)

INTRODUCTION

The River Meuse runs 900km from its source near Langres in France to the North Sea. After passing through Sedan and Charleville-Mézières just inside the French border it turns north into Belgium, through Dinant and Namur, then northeast to Liège after which it flows into Holland and becomes the Maas. It is navigable for a large part of its length, assisted in the more awkward stretches by canal constructions. However, even barges of up to 100m in length can pass Dinant and reach Givet in France. In the Ardennes area it's a grand and wide river with only a few bridges and the occasional ferry. It's seen at its best south of Dinant at Freÿr, where limestone cliffs tumble down impressively to the water's edge opposite the château of the same name with its elegant gardens.

DINANT

This very popular tourist town with the Meuse, the citadel, the church (Église Notre Dame) and Rocher Bayard, is distinctly photogenic. It makes a worthwhile visit but perhaps only once. As a destination in its own right it has heavy traffic, difficult parking and, in truth, not too much of great interest. However, it is fun to seek out the statue of Dinant's most famous son, Adolphe Sax; some will enjoy the cable car ride up to the citadel and a boat cruise up the river on a fine day is undoubtedly pleasurable.

The town has a colourful though very tragic military history. In 1466 it was burned by Phillip the Good, Duke of Burgundy, and his son Charles the Bold following an uprising against their

The attractive waterside view of Dinant

rule. As an added disincentive to future revolt some 800 souls were thrown into the Meuse and drowned. The 16th- and 17th-century wars between France and Spain led to occupation by different forces and great hardship. In August 1914 over 600 inhabitants were executed by Saxon troops of the German Army, allegedly as a reprisal for shots fired at soldiers repairing the bridge over the Meuse.

The Lesse is a significant tributary of the Meuse, the confluence at Anseremme being just over 4km south of Dinant. The highly scenic lower reaches offer some of the best walking and photographic opportunities of the Ardennes. The railway line connecting Dinant with Bertrix and Libramont runs through the area, and the two stations at Gendron-Celles (the villages of Gendron and Celles are both fairly close) and Houyet owe their continuing existence to the large volume of traffic generated by walkers and, more particularly, canoeists who use the river and its banks for their recreation. There are numerous possibilities for walkers to plan routes and explore the river; a base at Dinant, Rochefort or any of the villages in between is ideal for exploring the area.

WALK 22
The Meuse and the Lesse

Start/Finish	Place Baudouin, by the church in Anseremme
Distance	8.5km
Ascent	140m
Time	3hrs
Map	Houyet, Vallée de la Lesse (1:25,000)
Refreshments	Shops and eateries in Anseremme
Access	Anseremme is 3km south of Dinant on the N95

A great walk along the riverbanks of the Meuse and its much smaller tributary the Lesse, journeying through the impressive rocks of Freÿr with views to the opposite bank of the Meuse and the equally impressive gardens of the Château de Freÿr.

Opposite the kayak rental establishments in Place Baudouin in **Anseremme**, a path leads down to the bank of the **Meuse** and under the railway bridge. Here the river is very wide and navigable to quite large craft from pleasure boats to barges. The path passes a beautiful 17th-century house and the impressive priory before reaching the bridge over the entrance to the marina. Go straight ahead here, with tennis courts on the left, until a garden fence impedes further progress and steers the path to join a road.

Turn right and follow the road to its end where GR signs appear. Ahead is a path that keeps very close to the river and soon reveals good views of the **Château de Freÿr** on the opposite bank.

> The **Château de Freÿr** was originally just a keep, destroyed in 1554. In 1571 the first part of what can be seen today, the east wing, was constructed and in the 17th century the now familiar square shape was completed. It has been owned by the Dukes of Beaufort-Spontin since 1410 and the castle, along with its famous gardens and mazes, is open to the public.

Château de Freÿr

The path runs around the base of the Roches de Freÿr, which are much frequented by rock climbers, especially on fine weekends. A fork in the path offers the opportunity of climbing up leftwards, winding quite steeply through the woods and gaining over 100m while doing so. Predictably it emerges on the **N95**, blessedly almost opposite a café.

Passing (or leaving) the café, it's only a short walk S along the main road before taking a left turn into a country lane with an old and impressive fortified farmhouse, then easing down through a veritable tunnel of trees into the Lesse valley. Turn left at the bottom and walk for 400m to the bridge. Instead of crossing go down left and find a path that runs along the river all the way back to **Anseremme**.

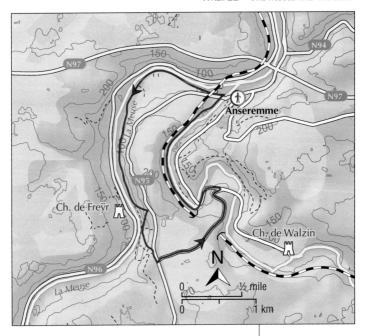

On reaching the outskirts stick to the water's edge all the way to the bridge where steps go up to the road. Turn left, et voilà – le parking.

WALK 23

*Gendron-Celles station to
Houyet along the Lesse*

Start	Gendron-Celles station
Finish	Houyet station
Distance	8.5km
Ascent	150m
Time	3hrs
Map	Houyet, Vallée de la Lesse (1:25,000)
Refreshments	Restaurant at Gendron-Celles station and cafés in Houyet
Access	Leave a car either at Houyet, as described here, or at Gendron-Celles if you prefer to walk in the opposite direction. Houyet is about 20km southeast of Dinant, reached by the N94, turning west onto the N929 some 5km after Celles. Alternatively, use Dinant as the start point for the outing and use the train outward and return.

To enjoy this walk to a maximum, hop on the train at Houyet, get off at Gendron-Celles and walk back. The path is sometimes narrow and grassy, sometimes a broader track; often it follows the water's edge but then climbs up above small crags. There are stony beaches on which to sit and listen to the sounds of the stream. Bring a picnic. Idyllic.

> *There is nothing more enjoyable in the Ardennes than the upper Lesse valley.*
> Percy Lindley, *Walks in the Ardennes* (1890)

From **Gendron-Celles**, leave the station (which is about 2km west of Gendron village and joined to it by a steep winding road) and stay on the same (E) side of the river. The level path heads off S and is marked throughout by a green diamond and by GR (126) signs, although the stress level for navigation on this route is almost zero (following the path nearest the water will nearly always pay off).

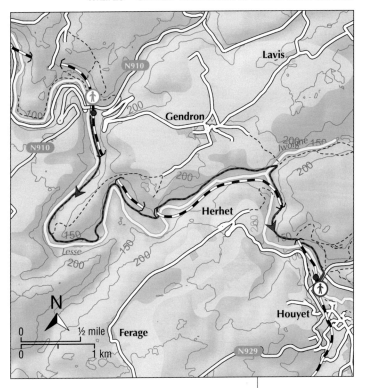

As you set off note the elongated campsite on the opposite bank which, together with its twin just before Houyet station, is full to bursting in July and August. At 2km you reach a track junction; the left-hand option climbs up to Gendron village, but you need to keep right. This stretch of river is particularly good for patrolling kingfishers, so when you are close to the bank keep your eyes peeled for that brilliant flash of azure as it does a low-level pass over the water.

At about 3km the path climbs steeply up through woodland where the riverbank is too precipitous for safe passage. Once surmounted, go down the steep flight of steps to regain the stream instead of being distracted by the broader track just above.

Inevitably, from time to time the route touches the railway – indeed, at about 4.3km, after passing under the railway bridge, you walk up a very steep path and arrive more or less on the iron road itself. There follows an interesting balcony path 40m above the river that includes a short ladder and handrails. The next landmark is the confluence of the Lesse with a tributary (the Iwoigne); the official crossing is via a dodgy bridge 100m upstream, but often you can jump or wade directly onto the path on the other side.

After 400m down what is now a broad track, a fascinating bit of history awaits. The railway has just re-crossed the river for the umpteenth time and just before you march underneath it you will see a track on the left going up towards the line. At the top is an old, barred and shuttered building. This was once the private station for the extraordinary Château Royal d'Ardenne.

The now disused station for Château Royal de l'Ardenne

Léopold II of Belgium succeeded his father in 1865. Although he was best known worldwide as the sole owner of the Belgian Congo, which he plundered mercilessly and cruelly, he was also a great builder and developer. On his father's Ardenne property here near Houyet he built the Tour Léopold (1878) close to the highest point of the estate. More dramatically he arranged for the construction of a huge Château on the site of an old hunting lodge. This was never intended as a residence but as a very grand luxury hotel, the intention being to attract the international nobility and the rich. It had an 18-hole golf course that still exists.

The **Château** was highly successful for a time but successive world wars led to its gradual decline, finally closing its doors in 1950 and being destroyed by fire in 1968. By 1970 it had been completely demolished. All that remains now of the royal plan is the Tour Léopold that serves as clubhouse of the Royal Golf Club du Château Royal d'Ardenne.

From the old station it's a short, flat stroll back to **Houyet** where crossing the river and railway returns you to the station.

WALK 24

Le Parc de Furfooz

Start/Finish	Car park at entrance to Parc de Furfooz
Distance	3.5km
Ascent	100m
Time	2hrs30min
Map	Houyet, Vallée de la Lesse (1:25,000)
Refreshments	Small buffet on riverbank (seasonal)
Access	From Anseremme go 5km east southeast on a minor road through Dréhance village. The park is signed from the village of Furfooz.

This small and most excellent nature reserve, nestling in one of the many exaggerated bends of the lower Lesse, would be termed a Site of Special Scientific Interest (SSSI) in the UK and is managed by a non-profit organisation, l'Association Ardenne et Gaume. This is an enjoyable family outing, although it is unsuitable for very small children. There are some very steep steps down a cliff face, albeit well protected by a handrail.

Furfooz Park is negotiated on a signed circuit starting behind the reception office. The small and cheap guide-book is in French and Dutch only but is worth having for the plan of the area even if you are not confident in either language. After just a few metres of climb you reach the Roman baths, the first of 10 defined points of interest that you will encounter (there are 13 numbered but these include things like the reception office).

This is a re-creation of **Roman baths** based on archaeological excavation of the original founda-tions. The scientific argument and discussion about these baths has been fascinating. Precise dating has understandably been elusive but the consensus is that construction took place in the second half of the first century AD. The water supply is problematic in terms of explanation; most believe there must

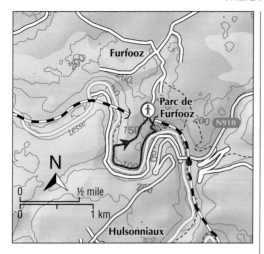

have been an underground spring but this is still uncertain. Just above the baths are traces of Roman as well as medieval fortifications, so the proximity is reasonable.

The most dramatic descent is via the very steep steps into *Le Trou du Grand Duc* (Eagle Owl hole). At the foot you arrive at a large and sensibly protected hole in the cliff face, some 50m above the valley floor. This is worth the effort for the view is fine and the situation excellent. Peregrine falcons nest on the cliff.

The subsequent descent to river-level is spectacular and straightforward, albeit very steep in places. The path winds down the cliff face with steps and a confidence-boosting handrail, through trees to a sharp right turn. Here is the entrance to Le Trou des Nutons. ▶

A nuton is a reportedly mischievous imp known only in the Ardennes. Beware.

Around 1864 Édouard Dupont found evidence in this **cave** not only dating back to farmers of Neolithic times around 4500BC but to a much earlier time. It is thought that the artefacts belong to the Magdalenian people, widely spread across mainland Europe about 11,000 to 17,000 years ago and known to be hunters of deer, horses and other large mammals – notably reindeer. This was towards the end of the last Ice Age.

Somewhere between here and the next cave, the Trou du Frontal, some of the water of the Lesse passes beneath your feet on its underground journey.

This was another of Dupont's explorations, with some evidence from Roman times and a Neolithic **tomb** dating from about 2500BC.

Le Trou du Grand Duc (seen from Walk 25)

Once down at the Lesse there is a short walk S to a buvette (small refreshment facility) used mostly by paddlers and only open at certain times. Ask at reception beforehand if you plan on feasting there. Behind the buvette is the normal return path which is a simple woodland stroll punctuated by three more caves.

La Grotte de la Gatte d'Or is the first of these. It is unusual in that visitors with a torch and sensible footwear are allowed to explore it. The name of the cave tells you what to expect – a place that gathers drops of gold. Who knows, you might be lucky and discover the treasure alleged to have been hidden there: gold wrapped in goatskin.

Le Puits des Vaux is particularly interesting and lies across a small bridge close to the end of the walk, just after joining a path that rises up from the left.

Although descent is not permitted into Le Puits des Vaux it contains a very deep lake with extensive subterranean spread, no bottom being reported at 30m by divers. This cave has been shown to be connected both to *Trou qui Fume* (the Smoking Hole) and to the Lesse. Fluoroscein studies have suggested a 70-hour transit time for water entering the system to regain the main river.

The Trou Reuviau lies a short distance further on just before the car park and reception area.

WALK 25
Château de Walzin

Start/Finish	Gendron-Celles station
Distance	11.5km
Ascent	200m
Time	4hrs
Map	Houyet, Vallée de la Lesse (1:25,000)
Refreshments	Restaurants in Furfooz village and at Gendron-Celles station
Access	From Dinant use the N94 to Celles (10km) and turn right onto the N910 to the station (4km).

An almost circular walk along the Lesse from the station to a truly magnificent and scenic castle, sadly not open to the public, set some 50m above the river.

Leave Gendron-Celles station, cross the river and after leaving the bridge leftwards go back under it on a surfaced lane. This is driveable as far as the hamlet of Chaleux. Although the walks in this book were designed to avoid tar as far as possible, in this instance it makes for a good walk, sunny in the morning and rather more open than on the opposite bank. Also, a river running close by distracts from the walking surface with its colours, shadows and music.

Soon after the start look over the water to the large limestone cliff of the Furfooz nature reserve where you can identify the exit of the Trou du Grand Duc (Walk 24). There is a picnic site for motorists after 1300m.

Where the Lesse turns north, note paths going left towards the village of Hulsonniaux. Almost 1km further on go under the railway bridge.

Alternative start without road-walking
This route is a little longer and somewhat rougher underfoot but with no road-walking.

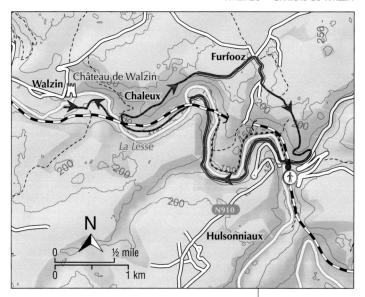

Follow along the river from the **station** (without crossing the bridge), passing the riverside buffet in the Furfooz nature reserve. Be careful not to miss the sudden left-hand turn on a small path into thick woodland just after a small dwelling. Then cross the river on the footway beside the railway bridge to join up with the road and the main route. ▸

Footways beside the railway are a helpful feature of the area, but would probably not be permitted in UK on health and safety grounds.

The road ends in the hamlet of **Chaleux**, where you ignore the road on the left and continue ahead until you might literally walk into the river. At the last minute turn left along the riverbank (bench, good picnic site); walk 80m and, after passing under the bridge, climb up the path to the railway line. Cross the river and descend at the end of the bridge so that now the river is on your left and the railway on the right. The path enters a veritable tunnel of trees (a bridle path runs parallel and is wider and usually drier) and continues for almost 1km before touching the river and reaching yet another rail bridge. Repeat the usual

151

trick to cross the river (using the railway) and on the other side duck under the bridge to pick up a very stony path with woods on one side and a nice meadow on the other. Very quickly the magnificent **Château de Walzin** comes into view perched high above the river, sitting on a vertical crag. Ignore a track that leads left to cross the railway and instead go downhill to the right, with good photo opportunities on the way down, to reach the edge of the river at the weir opposite the much-refurbished mill with the castle towering above you. Many people cross the river on foot here at low water-levels by using the weir or just paddling.

Château de Walzin

> The **Château de Walzin** was constructed in the 11th century and in its early days served as a surveillance post for the approach to Dinant from the south, sitting, as it did, squarely on the only ford for many miles. It was seriously damaged by French revolutionary troops in 1793 and restored to its current form in 1881. It is now a private dwelling, not open to the public.

Chaleux, seen on the return leg

It's just 800m of retracing your steps to the railway bridge to cross over to the east bank, then go under the bridge and past a cottage, very briefly N before curving round to a steady NE heading. This uphill wood-fringed stony lane is called the Rue de Chaleux and it leads to an exceptional viewpoint, 100m above the river, looking over **Chaleux** and a large loop in the Lesse. The lane later joins a track and continues over open ground to the top of the hill, descending on the other side into the village of **Furfooz**. Turn right at the T-junction.

Furfooz is a small, clean place with a good restaurant and craft workshops, both in the main (really the only) street of Rue du Camp Romain. Go past the church and take the zig-zag in the road downhill, then leave it by going up left into Rue de Molement. Just 20m up here turn left again onto a small track which leads up easily into fields, crossing a not very obvious spur before descending, ultimately quite steeply, to the N910. Gendron-Celles **station** is 300m down the hill.

WALK 26

Belvaux and the Bois de Niau

Start/Finish	Chapelle Saint Laurent in Belvaux
Distance	9.5km
Ascent	100m
Time	3h30min
Map	Rochefort et ses villages (1:25,000)
Refreshments	Restaurant close to the château near the halfway point; two restaurants in Belvaux
Access	Belvaux is 8km south of Rochefort and 2km south of Han-sur-Lesse. To reach the chapel from the road junction in the centre of the village go east, over the river and turn right. There is parking alongside a children's playground opposite the chapel and communal bread oven.

This walk traverses a variety of habitats from riverside to hilly woodland, culminating in a historically interesting old hermitage, currently the subject of an archaeological dig.

From the chapel in Belvaux take the path leading S, which soon reaches the riverbank. Here the Lesse is relatively slow-flowing but there are shallow stretches where it bubbles noisily over stones and it's a good place to see Dippers. The route here is easy and wide, rising up through the oak and beech woods interspersed with young rowan and hazel with some stands of conifer. The height gain is very modest and the way suitable for most people and children.

By the time you have walked 2.5km you are riverside again, although you might delay any refreshment stop until you are well clear of the *station d'épuration* (sewerage works). There is a huge old quarry just before the lovely road bridge over the river, with the **Château de Resteigne** immediately in front of you.

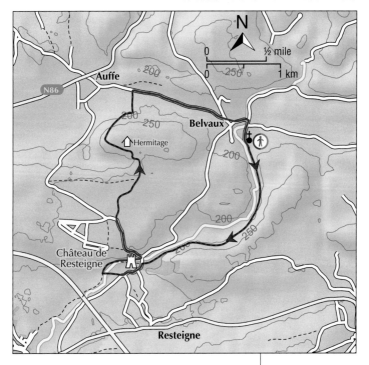

The imposing **Château de Resteigne** in its beautiful location dates from the 12th century, although what can be seen today was the almost new build of the 15th century, which has subsequently been changed extensively. It was the family home of the d'Hoffschmidt family for some time; these days it caters for business conferencing and family holidays.

Here you have the option of crossing the bridge and, with or without a pause at the conveniently sited restaurant on the opposite bank, continuing the walk or taking an additional small loop which adds only 1300m and passes the old water mill. For this, walk up the road to

The Lesse bridge

the left, keeping close to the château grounds, then take the right fork and keep right down to the lovely old house that was the mill. Here a wooden footbridge takes you over the river and you return to the main bridge on a nice path along the riverbank. There is no shortage of picnic spots thereabouts.

To continue on the 'main' route, go NW from the road bridge up the modestly steep road for 650m to a sign that includes direction to Ruines de l'Ermitage. Turn right onto this track that passes through open and wooded areas to a track crossing offering a choice of routes. Go straight ahead following the GR. On the correct route, after emerging from the trees, you walk along with a meadow on the right and forest to the left. Go up to a small clearing with a bench, path junction and signposts (Bois de Niau, alt. 200m). Turn left, still following the GR, continue for about 400m and reach another signpost.

A short diversion is important here: leave the route and go up the hill to the right for 50m and you will find the first part of the ruins of the **hermitage** of Edmond d'Hoffschmidt. This is what remains of a tower said to

THE HERMITAGE OF EDMOND D'HOFFSCHMIDT

Edmond d'Hoffschmidt (1777–1861), born into a noble Westphalian family, had been a young officer in Napoleon's army serving in northern Prussia and Jutland. He returned to his father's house at Resteigne after 1811 and decided to go into retreat as a hermit. He selected a site on the top of a hill in the Bois de Niau and there built a house, 'The Hermitage', living there for 15 years to meditate and worship nature and literature. Certainly it was a small dwelling by comparison with his home at the château, although maybe a little upmarket when set against most people's idea of the style in which a hermit might live.

While he was there he conceived a child with his 23-year-old house-keeper Victoire Suray, and a little girl, Léocadie, was born in April 1825. She, though not taking his name, was educated privately and expensively in Givet, Paris and Liège.

The hermitage in 1841

In 1830, after the death of his father, d'Hoffschmidt returned to live in the Château de Resteigne, occasionally spending time back in his retreat in the woods. He was very active locally and became the mayor in 1847, a post he held until his death.

have been 8.8m high. Around to the right there is the rapidly growing footprint of the main hermitage, currently the subject of a 'dig'. Visible in 2013 were the hall, cellar, stables, kitchen and bakery.

After visiting the hermitage, return to the path and the GR below. This winds steeply down through magnificent woodland, eventually reaching the edge of the trees where the path turns left through open country and down to the road. It is almost 2km eastwards along the lane and back through **Belvaux** to the chapel and parking area, passing en route Garage Lucy and, more importantly, a bar-restaurant on the left just before the river bridge.

WALK 27

Han-sur-Lesse and Rochefort

Start/Finish	Han-sur-Lesse tourist office
Distance	17km
Ascent	320m
Time	6hrs
Map	Rochefort et ses villages (1:25,000)
Refreshments	Plentiful in both towns
Access	Han-sur-Lesse is 6km south of Rochefort. From Dinant go east on the N936, south on the E411 (direction Rochefort and Luxembourg) and then left onto the N918 to Rochefort (38km).

This circular walk connecting the two principal centres of the Lesse-Lomme river complex is described from a start in Han, but obviously the same route can be followed from Rochefort. The excursion is not signed. For those preferring to start from Rochefort there is good, free parking some 400m down the N86 towards Jemelles at the roundabout at the foot of the hill.

HAN-SUR-LESSE

This village, 6km southwest of Rochefort, made its name, fame and fortune from the remarkable network of limestone caves that, although explored in the 18th century, took off as an international tourist attraction after 1830. The river Lesse disappears underground at the southeast corner of the Colline de Boine (the wooded hill south of the village) at a place called the Gouffre de Belvaux. It re-emerges on the north side of the hill at the Trou de Han, close to the centre of Han, having passed through at least 15km of galleries and halls even now probably not completely explored.

The guided tours of the system can be highly recommended to all fit enough to walk 2–3km underground (including a number of staircases). The temperature inside is a very comfortable 10–15°C. Part of the fun is the inclusive and historic tram ride from Han centre along the river and through ▶

the woods to the entrance at Gouffre de Belvaux. From the exit of the tour at Trou de Han it's just a short walk back to the village.

It's fascinating to note how the spelling of this small, often packed with tourists, little village has changed over the years, from the simple 'Ham' of 1139 to 'Hans-sur-Lesche' in 1266, followed by 'Han-sur-Lece' in 1465 and 'Ham-sur-Lez' in 1528.

For those seeking accommodation there is plenty on offer, although Rochefort offers a wider choice and is generally rather cheaper.

From the tourist information office in Han-sur-Lesse walk W along the main road and after 100m turn right just before the bridge over the **River Lesse**. Walk along the

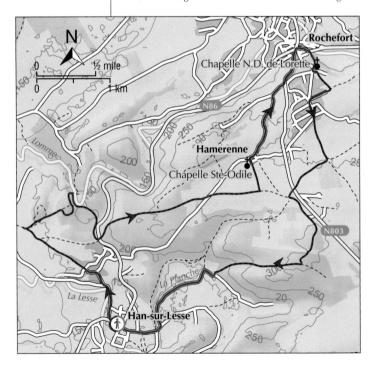

tree-lined promenade past the frequent benches. Across the water is a small campsite, one of several in the village. After you pass the weir the road rises up to a modern shrine to the Virgin Mary at a right-angle bend. Take the first turn right and then, at the T-junction ahead, go left into Rue de Malispré. When you reach a crossroads go straight over, the road becoming the Rue Dry Herleux. Walk past new houses before the tarred road becomes a track. Briefly join another tarred road (cross and bench) then 250m further on turn right onto an unsurfaced track.

The next section of the walk is known as the *Promenade sur les Traces de l'Ermite* (the walk in the steps of the hermit). As you walk past a wooded area on your left reach a fork where you keep right. This leads uphill into another wood. At the next fork keep left, soon emerging at a most excellent viewpoint peering down over a vertical rock face to the River Lomme far below. Litter dumping seems to be a problem here – a particularly sad sight in such a beautiful spot. Descend the steps on the left, which take you down the cliff very steeply but safely with a guardrail almost all the way.

Train to the Grotte de Han

On the way you pass the barred entrance of the **Grotte d'Éprave**. The official explanation is that entrance is not permitted to the public because of a particularly sensitive underground ecosystem, including bats and several species of spider. However, it is also a complex and difficult system, suitable only for experienced speleologists and expertly guided parties.

Immediately after the entrance to the caves go under a fine rocky arch and reach the bank of the **Lomme**. This is a particularly pleasant spot. Turn upstream along a good path and follow this along the riverbank, curving round to the left, soon leaving the river to cross the field and go up to the main road (N86). Cross directly (care required) to a steep, rough track that passes to the right of Bar-Restaurant Tamaris. Towards the top of the first rise go straight on at the junction and from there deviate neither left nor right, whatever the temptation, eventually leaving the woodland to cross open land to a tarred road. Cross over to another track that winds gently around a small hill and turn left at the first opportunity after that

Chapelle Ste Odile at Hamarenne

(unsigned). As you descend easily towards the first houses of the hamlet of **Hamerenne** you pass the white **Chapelle Ste Odile**. Turn right onto the tarred road and after 50m take the left fork.

> **Ste Odile** is the patron saint of good eyesight. Blind from birth, she lived an almost entirely monastic life, probably from AD662 to 720. The chapel was dedicated to her in 1714 or 1715.

From here the walk is on surfaced roads for the whole of the short distance into Rochefort. The navigation is easy. Bear right at the unnamed church and descend to the N803 where you turn left and go down to the beginning of the main street in **Rochefort** at the junction where the N803, N86 and N949 all meet (9km, 200m ascent so far).

ROCHEFORT

This is good centre for exploration of the Lesse valley, although, depending on the itinerary, some visitors will prefer to stay nearer the lower reaches of the river. It's an attractive, hilly town sitting above a loop in the River Lomme – a tributary of the Lesse. Its wide range of facilities includes a good tourist office in the main street, Rue de Behogne, which is also the N949. The feudal castle dating from the 11th century and the Trappist beers produced in the nearby monastery are well-known attractions.

The other tourist draw is the Grotte de Lorette; this series of caverns and passages carved out of the limestone by the Lomme is not quite as famous as the system at neighbouring Han and so tends to be less busy. It is equally spectacular but rather colder and has many more steps, enough to make it a bit of a workout.

The return trip to Han starts at the same road junction. Walk down the N86 (signposted Jemelle) for 200m and just before the bridge over the River Lomme take the track on the right. Go along this for just 150m to a ruined building and turn right; go up a few steps then immediately left. You are now walking along a small woodland path parallel to the track. Go up another flight of steps on

The explanatory plaque at Notre Dame de Lorette

MONUMENT CLASSE
Selon la légende
Josine de la MARCK
comtesse de Rochefort
morte en odeur de sainteté en 1626
ayant vu son jeune fils emporté par un singe sur les
toits du château, fit le vœu de bâtir une chapelle
si l'enfant échappait au danger.
Le chœur est la fidèle reproduction de la
Sainte Maison de Nazareth transportée par
les anges de Lorette en Italie.
Notre-Dame de Lorette,
Patronne des aviateurs,
PRIEZ POUR NOUS

the right and turn left at the top before zig-zags take you up to another junction. Here go right and uphill, partially surfaced and with a low wall, to emerge at a **chapel**.

The otherwise unremarkable **Notre Dame de Lorette** has an extraordinary story explaining its origin. Josine de la Marck, Countess of Rochefort, was the mother of a small boy who was taken by a monkey up onto the roof of the nearby Château de Beauregard. As you do, she made a vow that if the child survived she would build a chapel in thanks for presumed religious intervention. Most visitors will have the same unanswered questions: what was a monkey doing there in the first place and how did the small child get down safely? The chapel was founded in 1625 but the generous Countess died just a year later.

Continue W to pass the car park for the Grotte de Lorette, but before reaching the crossroads turn left up a woodland path (GR) and go up this for 350m to a cross track. Here turn right onto a tarred surface and walk to the crossroads. Now go left (S) into the Rue de la Croix St Jean and go up to the top of the rise. The newly renovated (2005) and rather unremarkable Croix St Jean stands here, now set among architecturally unusual and expensive-looking housing. At last you reach the countryside, going S on the small stony lane as far as a crossroads by a building where you turn right and continue to the crossing of the main road (**N803**). Go directly across to reach a track crossroads. You would be forgiven a moment of déjà-vu here when, if you glance 500m west, you will see a small hill and track very much like those you passed on the outward leg. Indeed it is the same place.

A small path goes left here and runs down parallel to the main road. Ignore the path on the left leading to the road and continue alongside more woodland, curving into it just before a farm. At a small clearing go downhill and turn right at the subsequent track crossing. Just 200m down from this, at a complex junction, go ahead but to the left (W) leading into an increasingly steep-sided and narrow valley with high ground on the right and a stream bed (often dry) on the left. The path ultimately curves down alongside a meadow to a road.

Turn right and follow the road down alongside the tiny **Planche river**. At the T-junction turn right across the bridge and back into **Han-sur-Lesse**.

WALK 28
Château de Montaigle

Start/Finish	Draisine (rail-bike) car park
Distance	8km 'cycling'; 3.75km walking
Ascent	Negligible
Time	1hr total on rail-bike; 1hr walking (plus castle and waiting time)
Map	Anhée (1:25,000)
Refreshments	No facilities
Access	Drive into the Molignée valley for about 3km until the second crossing of the old railway line, now a RAVeL. The car park is on the left.

This route entails a very short walk indeed, but the outing as a whole is such fun that it demands inclusion. Fitness may be required initially and the castle is a cracker. The Molignée valley railway branch line from Anhée to Ermeton-sur-Biert closed in 1962.

The river Molignée runs east along the **Molignée Valley** to join the Meuse between Anhee and Yvoir, about 7km north of Dinant. The valley is, for the most part, narrow and wooded, enclosed by limestone cliffs and buttresses and, apart from its surface, probably has changed little since 1880 when Katharine McQuoid journeyed this way.

In the car park get your ticket for the Draisine (rail-bike). For newcomers, a Draisine is a four-wheeled vehicle running on standard gauge rail lines and propelled by a tandem arrangement, one person each side at the front end. In between the riders and slightly behind them is a double seat from which passengers can exhort the pedallers to greater efforts (or act as reserve muscle). You travel at your own speed, although if you are very fit there is considerable advantage in starting with no one in sight

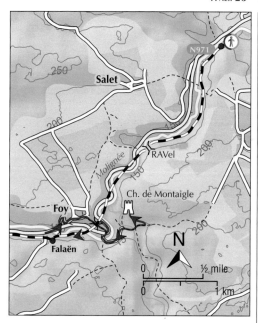

in front of you. These machines are very low-geared, so achieving 15km/hr is challenging.

So off you go. The single-track line (historically double-tracked) goes with only a slight gradient up the valley, through two tunnels and over many bridges (almost all double-arched traversing river and road), reaching the old station of **Falaën** after 4km. Here you dismount and confirm the time slot for the return trip to avert head-on collisions.

Go onto the main road, turn right (E) and walk down 80m to a road junction. Here follow signposts for **Foy** and keep right through that village until it's possible to bear right into a lane, soon becoming a track leading down a spur with the railway tunnel beneath your feet. When it reaches the main road take the small road almost opposite leading to some houses. Keep left and follow the road to the gate of **Château de Montaigle**.

Ruins of Château de Montaigle

This, the old **Montaigle castle**, dates from the beginning of the 14th century and was enlarged and modified considerably in the 15th century when it became an important residence. It was burned down by soldiers of Henri II of France in 1554 and never rebuilt. Essentially these are the ruins one sees today. However, after the local population started using the stone for their buildings, it was 'saved' in 1865 and significantly restored from 1982. There is an excellent English-language written guide included in the entrance fee, and a small museum with very interesting photographs. The entrance fee is reasonably priced and good value.

After visiting the castle return to the main road and with great care walk right around the large bend and under the railway bridge. On the left is a flight of steps that leads to the railway. Walk through the tunnel and back to **Falaën station** along the walking and cycle track that runs alongside the line. All that remains then is the mildly downhill cycle back to the **car park**.

5 LA ROCHE-EN-ARDENNE

Along the Ourthe (Walk 30)

169

INTRODUCTION

All at once we turn the corner of a hill, and there is the swift Ourthe winding round, and then curving out again, with the houses of La Roche built beside it, and the dark ruined castle, black as night, rising up from the rock on which it stands, in the middle of the town, frowning down, as it has done for centuries, over the meeting of valleys, in the centre of which stands the little town, the heart of the Ardennes.

Katharine Macquoid, *In the Ardennes* (1880)

At first glance this picture-postcard village would seem to have changed little in the 130 years since *In the Ardennes* was written.

However, bearing in mind that 90 per cent of La Roche's buildings were destroyed in two weeks during the German Ardennes offensive at the end of 1944, it is apparent that today we see a completely rebuilt town – albeit done very tastefully. The castle, originally built in the 11th century, still has remnants of towers, decent walls, an oubliette and so on, but was substantially damaged by shelling. Apart from a highly competent war museum the other wartime relics are a US Sherman tank on the Quai d'Ourthe, and a British M10 Achilles tracked tank destroyer with a 17-pounder gun up above the town by the Hotel du Chalet.

In addition to the town's splendid situation, the newly built park is beautiful and there are sporting and other entertainments to cater for most tastes. So the crowds still flock into town in July and August just as they did from Brussels and Liège in the 19th century. Kayaking, riding, walking and just plain relaxed tourism is the order of the day.

For some people, however, no matter how clean and neat, the town may be just a little too 'touristy'. It seems that every other shop sells souvenirs, cured ham, sausages or chocolate and there are enough restaurants to make your head spin. There are many advantages to visiting in June or September, if that can be arranged.

Whether it is a great rather than a good walking centre is open to debate. There are certainly some excellent walks and they are included here, although it doesn't compare with, for example, the Semois around Bouillon, the valley of the Lesse or the Hautes Fagnes.

WALK 29

*Maboge, Borzée and the ridges
above the Ourthe*

Start/Finish	Place du Bronze in centre of La Roche-en-Ardenne
Distance	15.5km
Ascent	350m
Time	4hrs
Map	La Roche en Ardenne (1:25,000)
Refreshments	Plentiful in La Roche; cafés in Maboge and Borzée (weekends only)
Access	La Roche is 66km by road from Namur (N4) and 70km from Liège (E25).

This is an opportunity to walk the high ground above the Ourthe through a variety of rural, almost lonely, habitats. The way is signed as local walk '6'.

Leave La Roche from the Place du Bronze at its NE corner and immediately turn right into Rue du Bon Dieu de

A welcome sight at Borzée – if it's open

Coming down into Maboge

Moka, which leads uphill quite steeply. The tarred surface is an inevitable but easy way to leave town; it continues as far as the hotel Domaine des Olivettes with its macabre history of being on the site previously occupied by the town gallows. About 800m further on the track forks at the place known as *Cresse de Corbeau* (crow's rock), allegedly where crows and ravens came to feed on the bodies of those executed by hanging, although local history does not relate why on earth the authorities would wish to move corpses almost a kilometre up the hill from the execution site.

Go left at the fork. Here, and throughout the walk, the way is very clearly signed. Soon the direction settles down to a steady SE along what is in effect a broad ridge, passing through a variety of woodland, scrubby cleared ground and, for the final 750m, agricultural land. Ignore the several side and cross tracks encountered. The next waypoint is a T-junction; turn left and after some gentle downhill walking through lovely woodland the track narrows to a path, veers right and plunges steeply down into

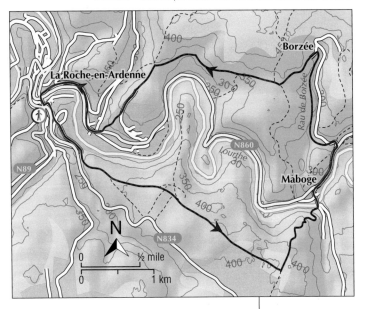

the Ourthe valley below, emerging at a road bridge in the village of **Maboge**.

After crossing the river into the village go up to the main road and turn right to follow it for 600m. Then turn left into a smaller road that goes downhill to cross a small stream towards the village of Borzée. Just a few metres after the bridge the path leaves the road on a track on the left. Go right and uphill at a fork and walk N up the valley. After crossing the small valley stream the path leads straight up to reach a road in the tiny hamlet of **Borzée**. This is true rural tranquillity with old houses, new houses, a delightful chapel and Le Clos René – the all-important refuge of the thirsty wayfarer. But higher up on the east of the village is a genuine carbuncle on the face of the countryside: the apparently abandoned 'Centre Nature'. So don't look back as you leave.

There is only a short uphill section SW on a track before the route levels off and then begins to descend more or less W. There are a few junctions and all are clearly signposted. From time to time there are stunning views to the south over the rolling and wooded hills so typical of the area. The obvious turn to the SW signals the start of the final section down to the valley floor; the surface is newly tarred, the houses expensive, the locality peaceful. Look out for the small path down to the right that cuts off a corner.

Walk towards La Roche on the N860 for a few metres and, just before passing the residence of the Gendarmerie National, follow the signs for walk 6 up to the right. Is this late height gain simply a main road avoidance scheme dictated by health and safety requirements? On the contrary: it gives great views of the town and passes some architecturally fascinating house designs, often with superb gardens, bringing you down past the delightful park to the river in the centre of **La Roche**.

WALK 30

The Celtic fort

Start/Finish	Bérismenil church
Distance	8km
Ascent	270m
Time	2hrs30min
Map	L'Ourthe Supérieure (1:20,000)
Refreshments	No facilities
Access	Bérismenil is 11km east of la Roche on the N860 and there is parking by the church.

Unreasonably little-known, this short tour takes in a partially restored Celtic fort on its journey through beautiful woodland, as well as a short ridge and a riverside ramble.

Almost opposite the church in Bérismenil is a tarred lane leading SW. Follow the local walk '6' with its yellow cross and keep left at the first fork, continuing to a small crucifix, the Croix sur Hache. Again fork left and walk down a grassy lane leading to a conifer plantation. Look out for a much smaller path going left, signed for Cheslé site Celtique, and follow it. A short distance downhill from here there is a map board at a path crossing. Go straight over and continue on path 9.

This narrow path climbs a low-relief ridge and twists and turns over outcrops where hands are needed for a tiny scramble. It passes a decent viewpoint; little can be seen of the river, just very steep-sided tree-covered valleys, which are impressive all the same. It ends all too quickly at the point where the entrance to the Celtic fort is being reconstructed.

This Celtic fortification seems to have served as a secure refuge to surrounding tribes around the fifth, sixth and seventh centuries BC. There has been quite a lot of digging and exploration, but the obvious

The Celtic fort

manifestations are the beginnings of reconstruction of the entrance to the fort and a very small portion of primitive rampart on two levels. The site is listed as a major heritage of Wallonia under the name of **La forteresse celtique du Cheslé**.

The path continues along the edge of the steepness above the river but is now on the flatter part of the spur that pushes into the wide loop of the Ourthe. It continues pleasantly and fairly level to the next piece of reconstruction – the defensive rampart. Just before this is a steep path (path 9) winding down to the river that is the next leg of the journey.

When it reaches the water's edge it joins the riverside path (path 6). Follow this left. It's not a place for fast progress but that offers time to watch the antics of the kayak crews, eyes ever alert for the elusive kingfisher and the best picnic spot. A tunnel of beech, alder and occasional sycamore keeps it pleasantly shady. When the river bend pushes the path E there is a junction; turn N up a steep and narrow (though shallow) valley to regain most

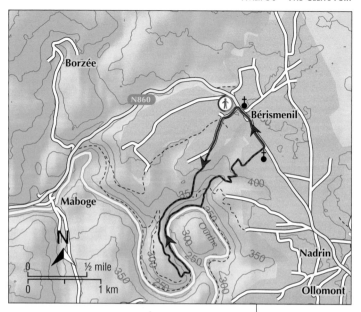

of the height lost on the descent to the river. Early on cross path 9 at the beginning of its journey from Nadrin to Cheslé and higher up traverse the tiny valley stream, the path becoming a wide track in dense forestry.

With several sharp turns this leads up to the **N860** main road at the pretty, 1882-built **Chapelle Notre Dame de Lourdes et Sainte-Gotte**. From there it's just 750m along the verge of the road back to the start in **Bérismenil**.

WALK 31
Circuit of the Lac des Deux Ourthes

Start/Finish	Dam parking area
Distance	14.5km
Ascent	500m
Time	5hrs
Map	L'Ourthe Supérieure (1:20,000)
Refreshments	No facilities
Access	Drive east from La Roche on the Houffalize road (N860) through Nadrin and at about 16km turn sharply right by an isolated house (signposted Nisramont). This road leads directly to the dam.

Generally, a walk around a reservoir does little to set the pulse racing with excitement, but this walk around Lac des Deux Ourthes (Lac de Nisramont, built between 1953 and 1958) is something of an exception. It is much more like a riverbank ramble, and indeed for much of the way follows the west and east branches of the Ourthe as well as paying a visit to their confluence. The signing of the route from the dam wall is done clockwise. Consider doing it anticlockwise as is described here, otherwise if the path is busy (especially with groups) it can be very difficult to pass if you are going more quickly than others. Don't underestimate the walk; the height gain is considerable even though it presents itself in small chunks.

The best place to begin this round-trip walk is in the dam car park at the north end of the lake. It's a deceptive start: after crossing the dam wall a well-surfaced, comparatively level, wide path leads down the W side of the lake, but reality soon kicks in with significant undulations and the height gain tally begins to tick up. A red diamond is the key directional symbol for the first section and these are so well-sited that no other instructions about avoiding other paths are required here. All along this bank there are small paths down to the lakeside where benches, sometimes tables, are provided for the picnic.

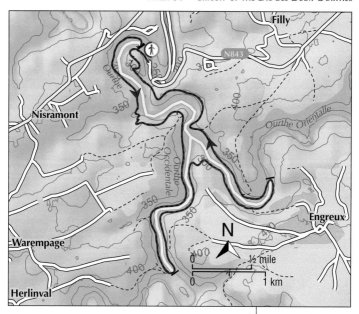

At about 2km cross a stream over a bridge notable for its name – Pont Rivière Kwai – which needs no translation for its humour. This is followed by one of the several short, steep ascents on the route that climbs over a spur and down to a small peninsula where the path turns S.

Soon, pass the **confluence** of Ourthe Occidentale and Ourthe Orientale before the path swings W and then S down to the bridge over the former, known as La Nasse de Berbret. Now beat up the E bank of Ourthe Occidentale without being put off by the signpost suggesting a wildly pessimistic 1hr back to the confluence. Keep riverside until you are forced uphill. This is a final pull up to the high ground above the confluence but there is no view to speak of. A few metres further on there is a large holiday complex with accommodation units looking down over the river.

*Confluence of
Ourthes Occidentale
and Orientale*

The way now leads back down to the river and SE before bending N to arrive at the bridge and weir of the **Ourthe Orientale**, La Nasse de Martimbay. The rest of the route becomes easier underfoot and reaches the biggest climb of the day, made much easier by flights of steps. From the top of the hill the last stretch back to the dam is an absolute delight; it includes a very narrow, steep-sided ridge, river on one side and road on the other, the path descending back to the dam **car park** through quite dense small oaks, sycamore and hazel, round corners, down steps – the lot. A great way to end a great walk.

WALK 32

La Roche, Cielle and Le Grand Bois

Start/Finish	Place du Bronze in the centre of La Roche-en-Ardenne
Distance	17km
Ascent	400m
Time	6hrs
Map	La Roche en Ardenne (1:25,000)
Refreshments	All facilities in La Roche; café-bar in Cielle and a café at the wildlife park
Access	La Roche is 66km by road from Namur (N4) and 70km from Liège (E25).

A great, though quite long, circuit starting in La Roche that largely avoids roads and visits the best woodlands in the area, finishing with super views over the town.

From the Place du Bronze in La Roche cross the Ourthe by the bridge in the centre of town, turn left onto the Quai de l'Ourthe and follow this to the next bridge. Cross this into Ave du Hadja and go up to the bend to follow GR signs as they branch right on a track, soon a small path in thick woodland. This leads round the loop in the river and picks up a road to re-cross the Ourthe to its N bank. A fair bit of the route from here up NW to the village of Cielle is on the road, but there is a handy shortcut through the woods to save some distance.

On arrival in **Cielle** go past the Relais de la Forge and the church and then up the aptly named Rue de la Chapelle to the **Chapelle Delacollette**. Next take the road right (NE) and consecutive right forks into the forest. In spring and summer the trees hide the ghastly quarry off to the east. It's almost consistently uphill for about 4km from the chapel until the point where a good track joins from the left. This is where a modest valley lies to the west, the other side of a newly planted plantation.

A view of La Roche

There is a five-way junction about 400m further on; turn 90° to the right and then immediately left (easy to miss but the signing is quite good). The next waypoint is a sharp bend in the path uphill to the left, followed quickly by a sign with the legend 'Nassché 515m'. This is where you leave the GR.

On the right is a small, unsigned path. Follow this SE then E for roughly 800m to a track crossing with an unsigned wooden post. Go down the track to the right, heading SW and downhill to cross a shallow valley before rising up to reach the N89 road west of Samrée. Cross the road and go through the gate to join local path 3. This wide forest track goes down through Le Grand Bois, crossing a tarred road before contouring around the left side of a large knoll. At the next path crossroads turn left, still following path 3, going quite steeply downhill to emerge on a surfaced road by an arboretum.

Turn right down the road, passing the Parc aux Gibier (the local **wildlife park** and a café), and just afterwards go left up a track. Cross the cattle grid and after 50m go down the small path on the right that leads into a very broad grassy ride. Follow this ahead for 350m and find a

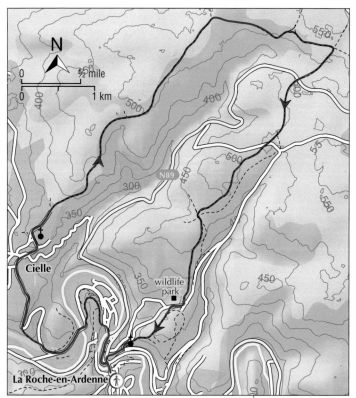

path leading down rightwards to a gate. Go through the gate and 200m down into the wood there is a wooden roofed viewpoint (Belvédère) with a splendid outlook over La Roche, probably the best around. Continue down on the right-hand of the two paths and within 150m arrive at a little whitewashed **chapel**.

The **Chapelle Ste Marguerite** was built in 1600 alongside the old road to Liège, close to a hermitage of which no trace remains. Local legend has it that a spring underneath the chapel fed the still visible

The Chapelle Ste Marguerite: the saint was the patron of pregnant women and newborn babies

water cistern of the castle. Sadly, the resident statues of Notre-Dame de la Douleur and Ste Marguerite were stolen in 1973 – a considerable disappointment to local women who, hoping to ensure a satisfactory outcome to their pregnancy, had traditionally invoked Ste Marguerite. The chapel is quite unusual with the right-hand wall being the schiste rock of the hillside.

Down the road from here is a hairpin bend; do not go round it – instead use the very small path that goes directly into the village, finishing down steps into Rue Gohette, which leads between the church of St Nicolas on the right and the castle high above on the left into the main street in **La Roche**. Cross this and finish the walk on the Quai de l'Ourthe or turn left in the main street and go back to Place du Bronze.

6 LUXEMBOURG

Clervaux's castle (Sentier du Nord, Stages 2 and 3)

INTRODUCTION

The Grand Duchy of Luxembourg measures just 82km north to south and 57km east to west. The part of the country north of a line drawn through Ettelbruck and Diekirch forms the outlying hills of the Ardennes.

The Grand Duchy is a veritable linguistic melting pot. French is the language of officialdom, used in political and legal papers as well as in the public services, but the everyday spoken language of the people at all levels of society is *Lëtzebuergesch* (Luxemourgish). Many public signs and street names are in this language. On trains the stations are announced with their Lëtzebuergesch names first and then in French. In his book *The Grand Duchy and its People*, published in 1913, George Renwick famously described the language as follows: 'Spoken, the patois sounds like curious Dutch and bad German coming from a worn gramophone.' This symbol of national identity is of Germanic origin and dates from around the fourth century, although many Germans do not readily understand it. German language signs on shops and restaurants are quite common and in the Luxembourg Ardennes, just as in Belgium, there is little English spoken.

Public transport is excellent and, notwithstanding the paucity of rail routes, there is an hourly service on every line, every day in normal working hours. Added to that is the advantage of a rail runabout ticket valid for a day at an extraordinary €4 (2013 price). The roads are very well maintained in this extremely clean country and in 2013 the price of fuel, especially diesel, was about 40 per cent cheaper than in the UK and other neighbouring countries, thus attracting 'fuel tourism'.

CLERVAUX

This highly attractive small town with its pedestrianised streets nestles among wooded hills in a hook of the River Clerve. Its centrepiece is the entirely rebuilt replica of its 12th-century castle that was almost completely destroyed during a spirited, and ultimately hopeless, defence by US troops at the beginning of the Ardennes offensive. It now houses exhibitions and a small but interesting war museum. The twin-towered church of Saints Côme and Damien shares centre stage, and dominating the forest skyline to the northwest of town is the 1909 Benedictine Abbey of St Maurice.

The town has all the usual facilities and a railway station on the line between Luxembourg and Liège.

WALK 33

The Sentier du Nord

The buildings of Féischterhaff above a loop of the Sûre

The Grand Duchy majors on long-distance paths. Although each town visited by tourists boasts an array of walks, many of them are very short or heavy on road use.

This guidebook takes the Sentier du Nord – the almost 70km north-south route from Weiswampach in the northeast of the country to Diekirch at the southern border of the Ardennes – as an example of what's available and attractive to walkers in this part of the Ardennes. In its entirety it's a terrific walk through almost all types of the region's terrain. Crucially, the path for much of its course lies close to a railway line and this allows for linear walks without transport difficulty.

Accordingly, for this book, each section of the Sentier has been allotted a stage number in its own right and is measured and timed between the relevant stations. Any of the walks can be combined to make a longer journey, although transport considerations often dictate the arrangements. The official signing throughout is the yellow diamond on a blue background (sometimes just a yellow diamond) – but note that on the official mapping it is in red.

Because the signage is so good throughout, generally only places of interest or importance and significant landmarks are included in the route description. Detail is given where the signs are poor or non-existent. Beware of the well-recognised medical condition known as 'straight-stretch hypnosis' where you settle into a rhythm on a path, enter a quasi-dream world and are blind to signs. This may be fatal to route-finding.

STAGE 1
Weiswampach to Troisvierges

Start	Crossroads in the middle of Weiswampach
Finish	Troisvierges railway station
Distance	9km
Ascent	125m
Time	3hrs
Map	Luxembourg R1 Clervaux – Huldange (1:20,000)
Refreshments	All facilities at both ends, nothing in-between
Access	To reach Weiswampach from Troisvierges for the start there are a number of buses operating daily from the railway station, many of which are timed to leave after the arrival of trains from Luxembourg. The journey time is around 20 minutes and in 2013 the service was operated by Voyages Stephany.

A very easy and pleasant country walk, this is the only section where there is no railway station at the beginning. Weiswampach has nothing of particular interest other than as a start point.

The route signs start in the middle of **Weiswampach** at the crossroads on the N7 and lead SW down the street, moving off the main road through some houses only to meet it again at the bottom of the hill. Turn right into a park area and continue along the lake, then rising up along the E side of a wood with the big leisure centre nearby. After the left turn into the woods the zig-zag course is easy to follow and ultimately leads to the main road between Weiswampach and Wilwerdange.

Turn right (W) for 300m along the road then go left into woodland. The track goes past a modest nature reserve and ultimately finds a main road again just NW of the hamlet of **Binsfeld**. After a short walk W down the road take the side road right, crossing a small stream, and go gently up through pastures on a pleasant track as far as the corner of a wood. Turn left and go along the wood to the road that leads down to **Troisvierges** past

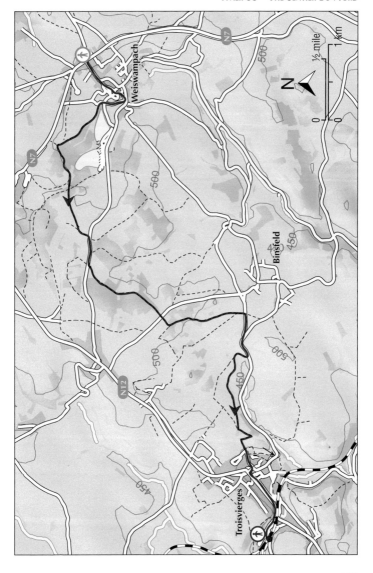

*The park at
Troisvierges*

the cemetery. On reaching the junction where the Sentier goes left towards the church, to reach the station go right then left down the main street (Grand-Rue) and fork left at the bottom.

To stay on the official Sentier route turn left and follow signs past the church and down a slight hill. There is a delightfully landscaped small park on the left that is a great picnic stop. The road rises up to the next landmark – the German artillery piece as described in Stage 2.

STAGE 2
Troisvierges to Clervaux

Start	Troisvierges railway station
Finish	Clervaux railway station
Distance	12km
Ascent	330m
Time	4hrs
Map	Luxembourg R1 Clervaux – Huldange (1:20,000)
Refreshments	All facilities at both ends, nothing in-between
Access	To reach the Sentier du Nord from the station, use the subway to emerge on the south side of the tracks. Walk to the end of the Rue d'Asselborn, go down the ramp and back under the railway on a footpath. Turn right and keep close to the embankment before walking through the campsite. Turn right again and cross the small stream, then go left along a grassy path that leads to a road. Just before the road turn sharply up right on a narrow path to climb over a wooded hill and descend the other side.

This is a particularly interesting section of the Sentier du Nord that embraces both a good walk and fascinating snippets of military history.

This section of the footpath starts in **Troisvierges** at the site of a WWII German 88mm PAK (*Panzerabwehrkanone*) gun, probably the most affective anti-tank weapon of the war, whose shell could penetrate armour as far as 2km away. From here follow the yellow diamond signs, starting by going along the road NE for just a few metres and slipping rightwards down a side road. At the top of the subsequent hill the road reaches 485m and the route turns sharply right down through woodland – look out for deer hereabouts – to reach the railway just before the hamlet of **Cinqfontaines** just across the Woltz river.

A little way down the track there is a good view of an **old convent** that has a grim history. In WWII about 700 elderly Jews were gathered here by the

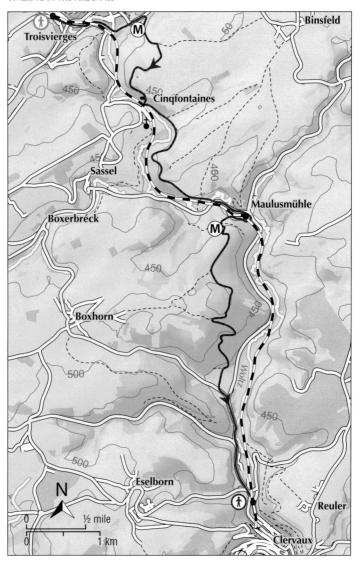

occupying German authorities, under the guise of it being a rest or old age home, and later despatched to Auschwitz and other concentration camps by train from the station, now closed, just below. Just above Cinqfontaines village there is a memorial at the roadside.

German 88mm anti-tank gun

Leaving this level section to climb through woodland again, go through two iron gates (signposted to Maulusmühle). It's about 2km to the next trackside walk by a level crossing gate. After 150m along the trackside path reach a road and turn left to reach the small village of **Maulusmühle**. There is poor signing here. Cross the Woltz and then turn immediately right across the railway track and go along the road running W parallel to the river for 350m. Then turn uphill on steep steps – the walker's nightmare – and follow signs up into the woodland to a very fine war **monument**.

There are six **graves** here. Three belong to the radio operator, navigator and gunner (two British and a New Zealander) of Lockheed Hudson FK803 of 161 Squadron RAF operating from Tempsford in Bedfordshire. The pilot, Flt Lt Helfer, had successfully baled out and survived the war. The engines and wings of the aircraft with a small piece of fuselage lie in a fenced-off compound by the graves.

161 Squadron RAF specialised in covert operations and this aircraft and its occupants, the other three being Belgian officers, were returning from the secret Special Operations Executive (SOE) Operation Benedict when, on the night of 20/21 March 1945, they were shot down by a night fighter. The memorial stone attributes this to Luftwaffe action but some later accounts say that it was possibly a United States Army Air Force (USAAF) aircraft.

Although there are several junctions and track crossings the remainder of the woodland route is straightforward, finishing across open land and going up to a road. Go left and follow this road, and those it joins, for the 1.5km walk to Clervaux **station**.

STAGE 3
Clervaux to Drauffelt

Start	Clervaux railway station
Finish	Drauffelt railway station
Distance	6.5km
Ascent	175m
Time	2hrs
Map	Luxembourg R1 Clervaux – Huldange (1:20,000)
Refreshments	All facilities in Clervaux; bar and Chinese restaurant in Drauffelt

A straightforward, well-signposted, delightful walk, largely through woodland.

Leave Clervaux **station**, heading towards town along the Grand Rue that continues as a pedestrianised street, curving right into the Place de la Liberation and crossing the river Clerve. There it joins the main road, Route de

Benedictine monastery of St Maurice

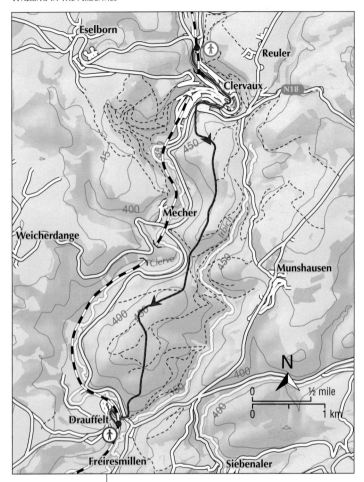

Marnach, followed up to its first sharp bend. Go straight ahead here (signposted Drauffelt) for just a few metres and then go up some steps on the left past the cemetery to arrive again on Route de Marnach. Now go into the entrance of St Francis' *maison de retraite* (nursing home), which gave a worryingly warm welcome to the writer. Up left there is a lane taking the route to a high point on the open ridge where it leaves surfaced roads behind until Drauffelt. Look back to see the impressive (albeit newish, built in 1910) Benedictine Abbey of St Maurice dominating the skyline to the north northwest.

The track gradually turns S and enters the forest. It's a delightful and easy-to-follow route, in woodland almost all the way except for occasional areas of logging and replanting. In places the map doesn't exactly portray the tracks on the ground, but as long as an eagle eye is kept for the yellow diamond signs all should be well. Ultimately a very small path drops down onto a road close to a junction. To reach Drauffelt **station** turn right and cross the river. To continue along the Sentier du Nord turn left and follow the signs.

STAGE 4
Drauffelt to Kautenbach

Start	Drauffelt station
Finish	Kautenbach station
Distance	13km
Ascent	350m
Time	4hrs30min
Maps	Luxembourg R1 Clervaux – Huldange (1:20,000);
	Luxembourg R2 Boulaide – Wiltz (1:20,000)
Refreshments	Bar and Chinese restaurant in Drauffelt; bar-café in Pintsch;
	pub in Lellingen; hotel in Kautenbach
Access	To join the Sentier du Nord from the station, cross the river eastwards and then follow the road south to where a small road joins from the right about 160m from the station.

This walk is harder than it looks on the map because of the height gain, but this is mitigated by refreshment possibilities en route and the option of a substantial shortcut.

From the Sentier du Nord in **Drauffelt**, cross the bridge over a small stream to the junction. The yellow diamond waymarks are unhelpful here. Go up the left, smaller, road for just a few metres then take the track/road leading uphill to the right. At the end of this road, by the cemetery, a path leads left for quite a pull up through the woods to open ground. After a pleasant walk over the crest descend to a road, turning right at the crossroads and easing down to another crossroads by an attractive shrine. Although this last section and the next, turning left to reach **Pintsch village**, brings with it almost 1.5km of road-walking, relief is at hand. As you reach a T-junction with the church on the left, just opposite the church is a bar-café. Try the croque-monsieur.

Back at the junction turn S down a lane and then sharply back right to enjoy the flat, grassy walk to the village of **Lellingen** – a delightful place that also has refreshment possibilities. The official route out of the

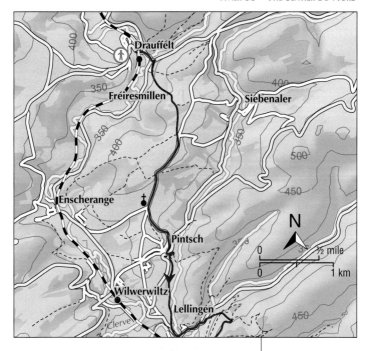

village is a puzzling choice although not unattractive. It leads up the valley NE and about 100m after crossing the valley stream makes a dramatic right turn on a barely visible path. A better path through trees crosses one forestry track and then reaches another. In 2013 the area ahead here had been felled and, presumably, so too had the signs. So cross the track onto a faint path and once back in the trees the signs resume to find a clever way around a cwm. On the next forest track turn right and here lies the puzzle, for it then steadily loses all that precious height gain to join with a path that has come directly from the village over a much shorter distance.

The next section is straightforward and includes a small deviation E to cross a stream and then a similar but

map continues on page 201

Chapel above Pintsch

larger excursion. Some 600m after this you reach a road. The Sentier takes you left up the road to visit the interesting-looking **Schuttbourg castle**, which dates from the 12th century and has been extensively restored following severe damage in WWII. Unfortunately it's private property and entry is prohibited. The alternative route, which was to turn right on reaching the road, quickly rejoins the official route and saves 800m. The committed long-distance path purist will no doubt follow the signposted route but there is a clear and persuasive choice.

Follow the road round to cross the Clerve by a most attractive old mill house and turn left. This good path entails more ascent, using in part a nature trail, and rises to a good viewpoint for Schuttbourg to the north

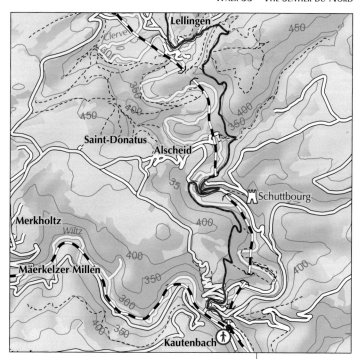

northeast. The steepish downhill section that follows mostly uses a lane to reach **Kautenbach village**. At the bottom keep right into the village proper and reach the Hotel Huberty. It's a really nice village centre with a small park alongside the Clerve immediately before its confluence with, and loss of its name to, the Wiltz.

Go E across the bridge and after 100m leave the Sentier du Nord by turning right for the station (signposted) on the road leading down to the river Wiltz. Go under the bridge and back left in a 270° turn to get onto the station platforms.

STAGE 5

Kautenbach to Goebelsmühle

Start	Kautenbach railway station
Finish	Goebelsmühle railway station
Distance	8km
Ascent	190m
Time	2hr30min
Maps	Luxembourg R2 Boulaide – Wiltz (1:20,000); Luxembourg R3 Diekirch – Putscheid (1:20,000)
Refreshments	Hotel in Kautenbach
Access	To join the Sentier du Nord from the station, first go through the subway to the car park. The road goes over the river alongside to the railway and then turns through 270° to go back under the railway bridge, rising to a busier road just east of Kautenbach village (600m).

One of the shorter sections of the path, this could reasonably be added to Stage 6 (although this would make for a tough day). In its own right a very pleasant little outing.

Having established yourself on the Sentier du Nord from Kautenbach **station** (see access note), go up the road (SE) to a sharp left bend. Take the small path that goes up steps directly ahead. When this path meets a road at the top of the hill turn right along it, signed appropriately with the familiar yellow diamond, and continue for 800m to where the Sentier leaves the surfaced road and turns sharply back SW. Gradually gain height to a viewpoint with a seat. The next feature to look out for is an extensive loop to the N in a narrow wooded valley, gloomy on a cloudy day. One might expect to cross the small stream and return on the opposite bank, but the route surprises by turning back on the same side and running downhill at the water's edge, to cross much lower down at a small plank bridge.

The best part of the walk now follows. The route rises quite steeply from the stream to cross a spur then

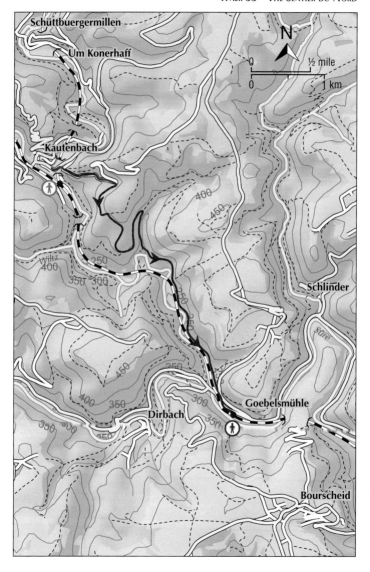

Often the path follows the railway closely

darts into a small re-entrant before climbing to another spur. This is a very attractive section. The tiny path winds around rocky outcrops and through the trees before it goes fairly gently down to **railway** level. After a stroll down a track you hit the surfaced road that rises slightly to join the main road. Goebelsmühle **station** is just ahead.

STAGE 6
Goebelsmühle to Diekirch

Start	Goebelsmühle railway station
Finish	Diekirch railway station
Distance	20km
Ascent	700m
Time	7hrs
Map	Luxembourg R3 Diekirch – Putscheid (1:20,000)
Refreshments	Hotel and bar in Lipperscheid, 500m off-route; all facilities in Diekirch

This is the longest and toughest portion of the Sentier du Nord. A drawback to what would otherwise be a splendid long walk is that there are four sections of road-walking, amounting to over 7km, although 4km of this is the final run down into Diekirch on attractive lanes.

Leave Goebelsmühle **station** down the road E, the yellow diamond Sentier du Nord signs in evidence after about 300m. Just past the road junction the path climbs steeply up left; it's a tough start, over 80m climb without relief, but once past the T-junction (turn right) the good path contours easily enough NE until a descent to a sharp turn to the E, and a metalled road heralds the appearance of the hamlet of **Schlinder**.

From there it's just 300m S to the main road. Turn left and walk down for 400m to find a path rising left up from the road.

The next part of the walk passes close to the village of **Lipperscheid**, some 500m off the route but a source of refreshment. It also includes the second of the road-walking stretches that finishes at the hamlet of **Dellt**. From here the track leads SW through open land before turning SE and up to the best **viewpoint** of the walk, especially for Bourscheid Castle which is seen frequently en route.

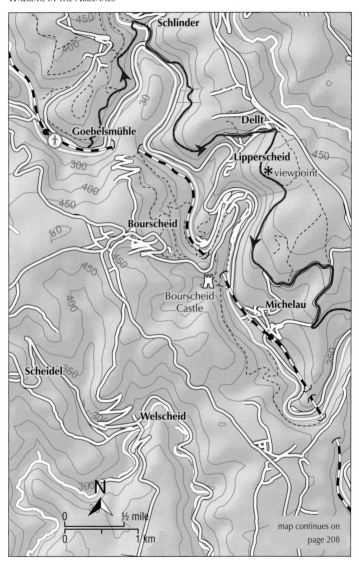

Schlinder

Goebelsmühle

Dellt

Lipperscheid

* viewpoint

Bourscheid

Bourscheid Castle

Michelau

Scheidel

Welscheid

N

0   ½ mile

0   1 km

map continues on
page 208

Bourscheid Castle, probably the best of its kind in Luxembourg, sits prominently on a spur dominating a big loop in the River Sûre. It dates from at least 1095, although it has since been significantly extended, and is open to the public.

Bourscheid Castle, sitting high above a loop in the Sûre

Care is needed after this. The path rises along a wood and arrives at a junction. **Do not** follow the yellow diamond sign indicating a left turn (in 2013 it was incorrect); instead keep right and 100m further on go right again, only signed for a local path, into the forest. Soon the signposting restarts and the path goes steeply down to join a road.

This is a fair stretch of road, reaching a high point of almost 420m at approximately the halfway point of the walk before leading down the spur towards **Michelau** – an escape route if you need its railway station. Before the road turns W towards the village make a sharp left turn onto a track. While walking from here through the woodland keep a good lookout for signs at the several junctions. Particularly, after crossing a small stream and

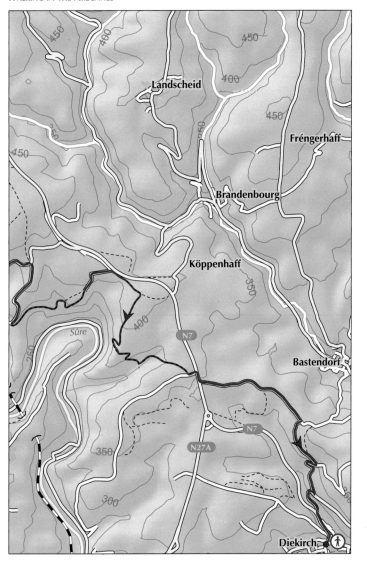

rising up the other side in a re-entrant, the sharp right turn is unsigned (in 2013). If you miss this, no matter: the steep track ahead rejoins the correct way at the top of the hill. Then it's straightforward to the point where you reach the main **N7** road.

Immediately after touching the main road the route leaves it, going past the farm known as Closdellt and after 100m branching sharp right (SW). There is a pleasant walk down along the edge of the woodland and, almost at the end of the open ground, a sign directs you into the trees. Immediately there is a signpost for *Predigstuhl* (**The Pulpit**). This steep little path goes down to a rather unimpressive viewpoint and then climbs back up almost to where you started. You may feel it's not worth the effort. It

209

can be avoided simply by continuing ahead for less than 100m and rejoining the route there.

Be careful to select the correct downhill path from here whichever option you choose. Although the correct route is well signed there is an alternative path, initially well worn, going downhill in the wrong direction. A compass check will give assurance that the correct path leads just S of E. Descend into a valley to cross a tiny brook, rising on the other side to the N7 again. Go right along the main road for 100m and then turn left onto a country lane. There is a right turn just after the first farm and then the same lane takes you down into **Diekirch** and past the military museum.

> **Diekirch** is a pleasant enough place with a smart pedestrianised area around the Place de la Liberation, but the real attraction for many is the huge and beautifully done military museum focussed particularly on the Ardennes battles of December 1944. This is a key visit in the area.

From the military museum go down Bamerthal and just past the church of St Laurent to the Place Guillaume – largely a car park in the Rue de Stavelot – where the Sentier du Nord ends. To reach the **station** continue S on Rue de Stavelot and turn right into Avenue de la Gare.

APPENDIX A
Route summary table

No	Start	Distance (km)	Ascent (m)	Time	Page
Bouillon and the River Semois					
1	Bouillon	24	400	8hrs	31
2	Corbion	15.5	650	6–7hrs	40
3	Poupehan/Bouillon	7.5/22.5	170	3hrs/6hrs	48
4	Vresse-sur-Semois	14.5	400	5hrs	52
5	Bohan	12	370	4hrs	58
6	Dohan	16.5	300	4hrs30min	62
7	Orval Abbey	7	100	2hrs	65
8	Herbeumont	9	175	3hrs	70
9	Herbeumont	19	380	6–7hrs	74
10	Bouillon	2	75	1hr	80
11	Bouillon	3.5	180	1hr30min	83
12	Bouillon	5	100	2hrs	85
Spa					
13	Solwaster	8.5	240	3hrs	87
14	Spa	13	280	3hrs30min	91

No	Start	Distance (km)	Ascent (m)	Time	Page
15	Spa	7.5/16.5	230/380	2hrs30min/5hrs30min	100
16	Spa	9.5	180	3hrs	105
Hautes Fagnes, Malmedy and Stavelot					
17	Baraque-Michel	13.5	120	4hrs30min	112
18	Nahtsief	17	170	4hrs30min	117
19	Auberge du Moulin de Bayhon	10	200	3hrs30min	122
20	Robertville dam	6.5	220	2hrs30min	125
21	Stavelot	22.5	600	7hrs30min	128
Dinant, the Meuse and the Lesse					
22	Anseremme	8.5	140	3hrs	139
23	Gendron-Celles	8.5	150	3hrs	142
24	Furfooz nature reserve	3.5	100	2hrs30min	146
25	Gendron-Celles	11.5	200	4hrs	150
26	Belvaux	9.5	100	3hrs30min	154
27	Han-sur-Lesse	17	320	6hrs	159
28	Les Draisines de la Molignée	3.75/11.75	negligible	2–4hrs	166

APPENDIX A – ROUTE SUMMARY TABLE

No	Start	Distance (km)	Ascent (m)	Time	Page
La Roche-en-Ardennes					
29	La Roche	15.5	350	4hrs	171
30	Bérismenil	8	270	2hrs30min	175
31	Lac des Deux Ourthes	14.5	500	5hrs	178
32	La Roche	17	400	6hrs	181
Luxembourg					
33	Sentier du Nord	(68.5)	(1870)	(23hrs)	187
Stage 1	Weiswampach	9	125	3hrs	188
Stage 2	Troisvierges	12	330	4hrs	191
Stage 3	Clervaux	6.5	175	2hrs	195
Stage 4	Draufelt	13	350	4hrs30min	198
Stage 5	Kautenbach	8	190	2hrs30min	202
Stage 6	Goebelsmühle	20	700	7hrs	205

213

APPENDIX B
Useful websites

Tourist information including accommodation

Wallonia general
www.belgiumtheplaceto.be
www.gitesdewallonie.be
www.allochambredhotes.be

Bouillon and the River Semois
www.bouillon-tourisme.be
www.ardenne-namuroise.be

Spa
www.spatourisme.be

Hautes Fagnes, Malmedy and Stavelot
www.malmedy.be
www.stavelot.be/tourisme

Dinant, the Meuse and the Lesse
www.dinant-tourisme.com
www.valdelesse.be

La Roche-en-Ardenne
www.la-roche-tourisme.com

Luxembourg
www.tourisme-clervaux.lu

Camping
www.eurocampings.co.uk
www.alanrogers.com
www.ukcampsite.co.uk (select 'Other Countries' to search for Belgian campsites)

Other information

Transport
www.b-europe.co.uk (website for SNCB – Belgian state railway)
www.infotec.be (for bus travel in Wallonia)

Cash passport

www.travelex.co.uk

www.cashpassport.com

Tourist attractions

Parc de Furfooz
www.parcdefurfooz.be

The Grotte de Han (cave system)
www.grotte-de-han.be

Les Sentiers de Grande Randonnée (information on long-distance footpaths)
www.grsentiers.org

Semois Kayaks (kayak and canoe hire)
www.semois-kayaks.be

Draisines-Railbike de la Molignée (rail-bikes)
www.draisine.be

Orval Abbey (Trappist monastery)
www.orval.be

Château de Rheinhardstein
www.reinhardstein.net

Montaigle (château)
www.montaigle.be

Château de Franchimont
www.chateau-franchimont.be

Diekirch National Museum of Military History
www.mnhm.lu

L'Ermite de Resteigne
http://ermitederesteigne.be

NOTES

NOTES

NOTES

NOTES

The Great Outdoors

DIGITAL EDITIONS

30-DAY
FREE TRIAL

- Substantial savings on the newsstand price and print subscriptions
- Instant access wherever you are, even if you are offline
- Back issues at your fingertips

Downloading **The Great Outdoors** to your digital device is easy, just follow the steps below:

The digital edition is also available on

The 30-day free trial is not available on Android or Pocketmags and is only available to new subscribers

 Available on Android   pocketmags.com

LISTING OF CICERONE GUIDES

For full information on all our
guides, books and eBooks, visit
our website:
www.cicerone.co.uk.

Walking – Trekking – Mountaineering – Climbing – Cycling

Over 40 years, Cicerone have built up an outstanding collection of 300 guides, inspiring all sorts of amazing adventures.

Every guide comes from extensive exploration and research by our expert authors, all with a passion for their subjects. They are frequently praised, endorsed and used by clubs, instructors and outdoor organisations.

All our titles can now be bought as **e-books** and many as iPad and Kindle files and we will continue to make all our guides available for these and many other devices.

Our website shows any **new information** we've received since a book was published. Please do let us know if you find anything has changed, so that we can pass on the latest details. On our **website** you'll also find some great ideas and lots of information, including sample chapters, contents lists, reviews, articles and a photo gallery.

It's easy to keep in touch with what's going on at Cicerone, by getting our monthly **free e-newsletter**, which is full of offers, competitions, up-to-date information and topical articles. You can subscribe on our home page and also follow us on **Facebook** and **Twitter**, as well as our **blog**.

Cicerone – the very best guides for exploring the world.

CICERONE

2 Police Square Milnthorpe Cumbria LA7 7PY
Tel: 015395 62069 info@cicerone.co.uk
www.cicerone.co.uk